EMOJI

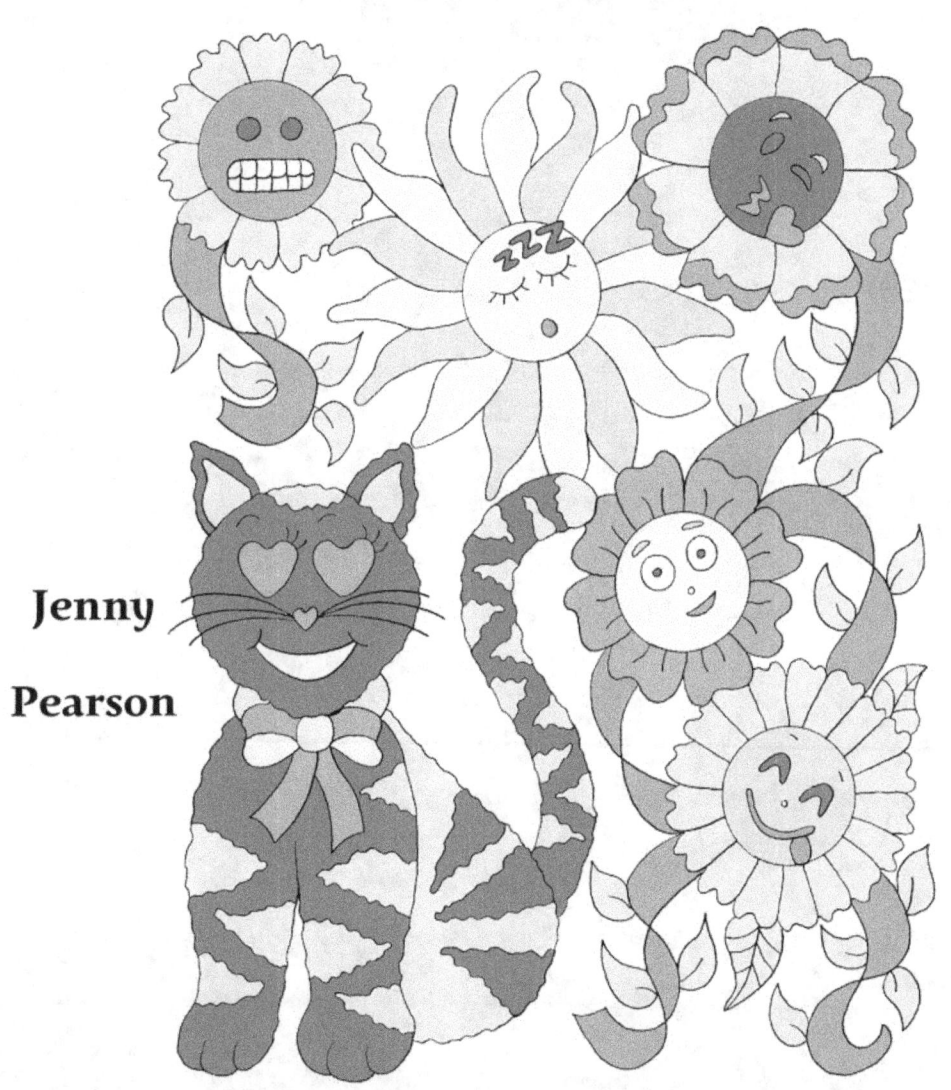

Jenny

Pearson

COLORING BOOK

Emoji Coloring Book
Coloring Fun for all ages

Jenny Pearson 97819836

Kivett Publishing
ISBN: 978-1-983-00728-6

Arts & Photography > Drawing > Coloring Books

INTRODUCTION

These designs are the creation of artist Jenny Pearson.

Sit back, relax, and relieve some stress. Enjoy!

Note: For those who prefer to color with markers, the back side of every page is blank.

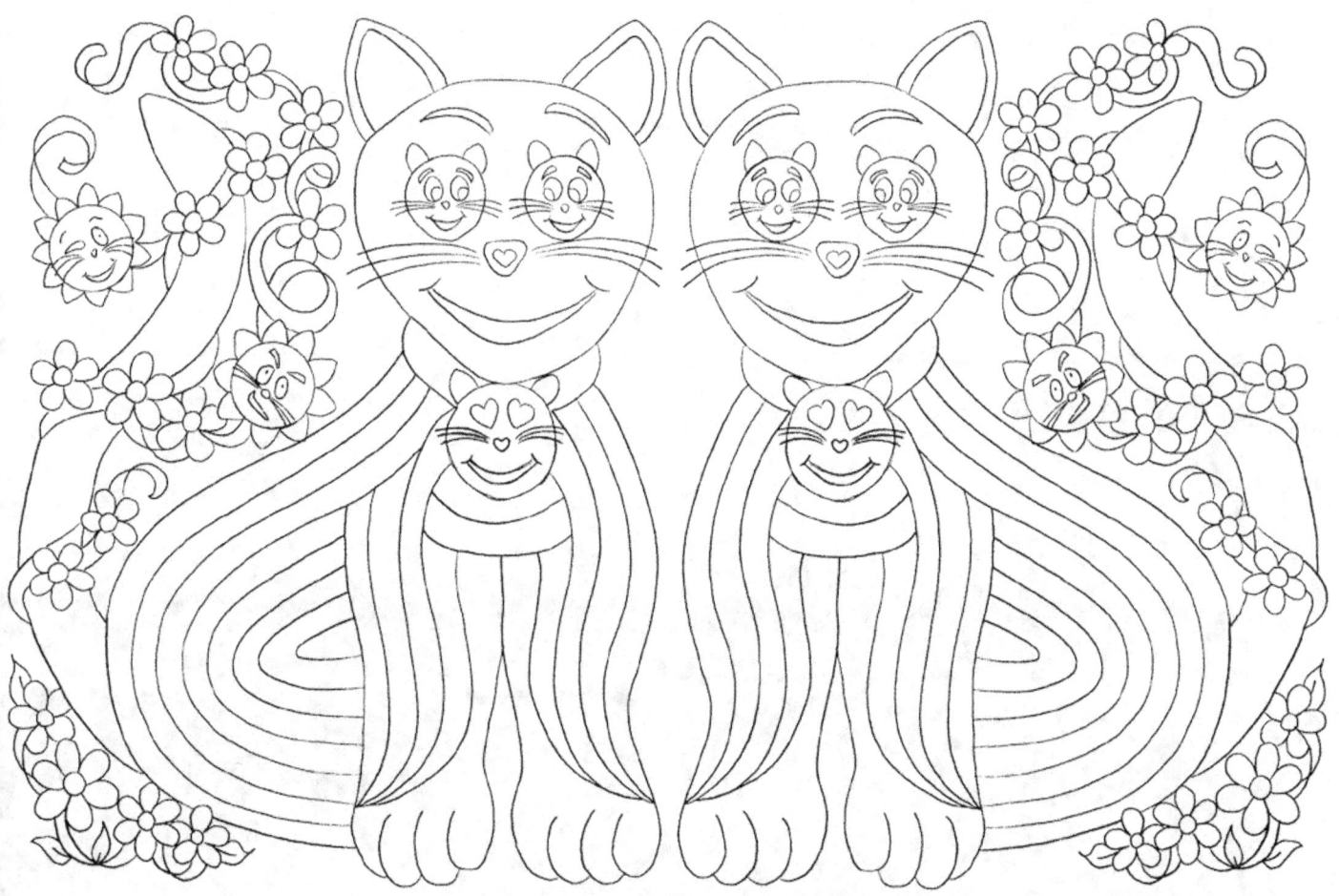

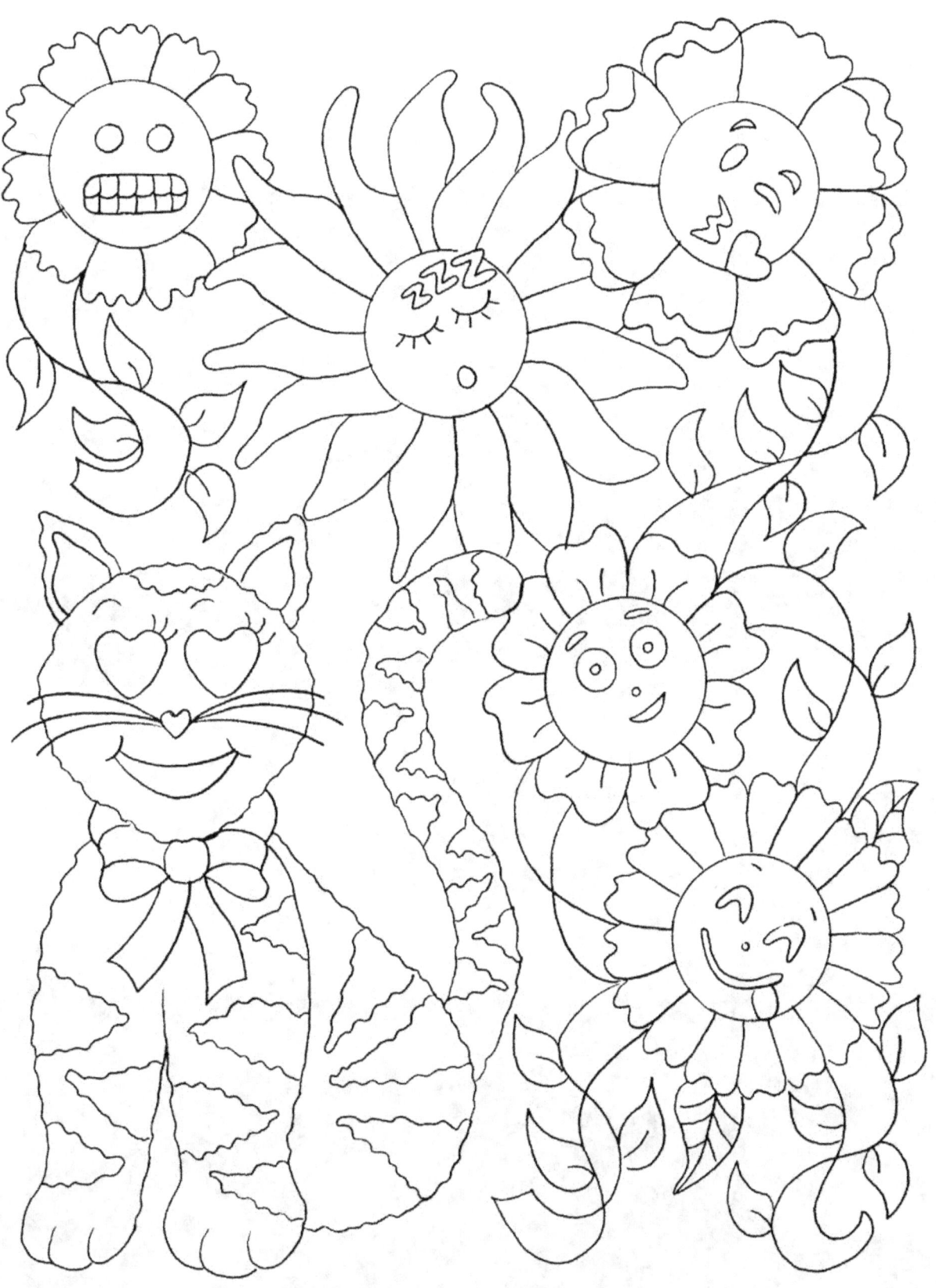

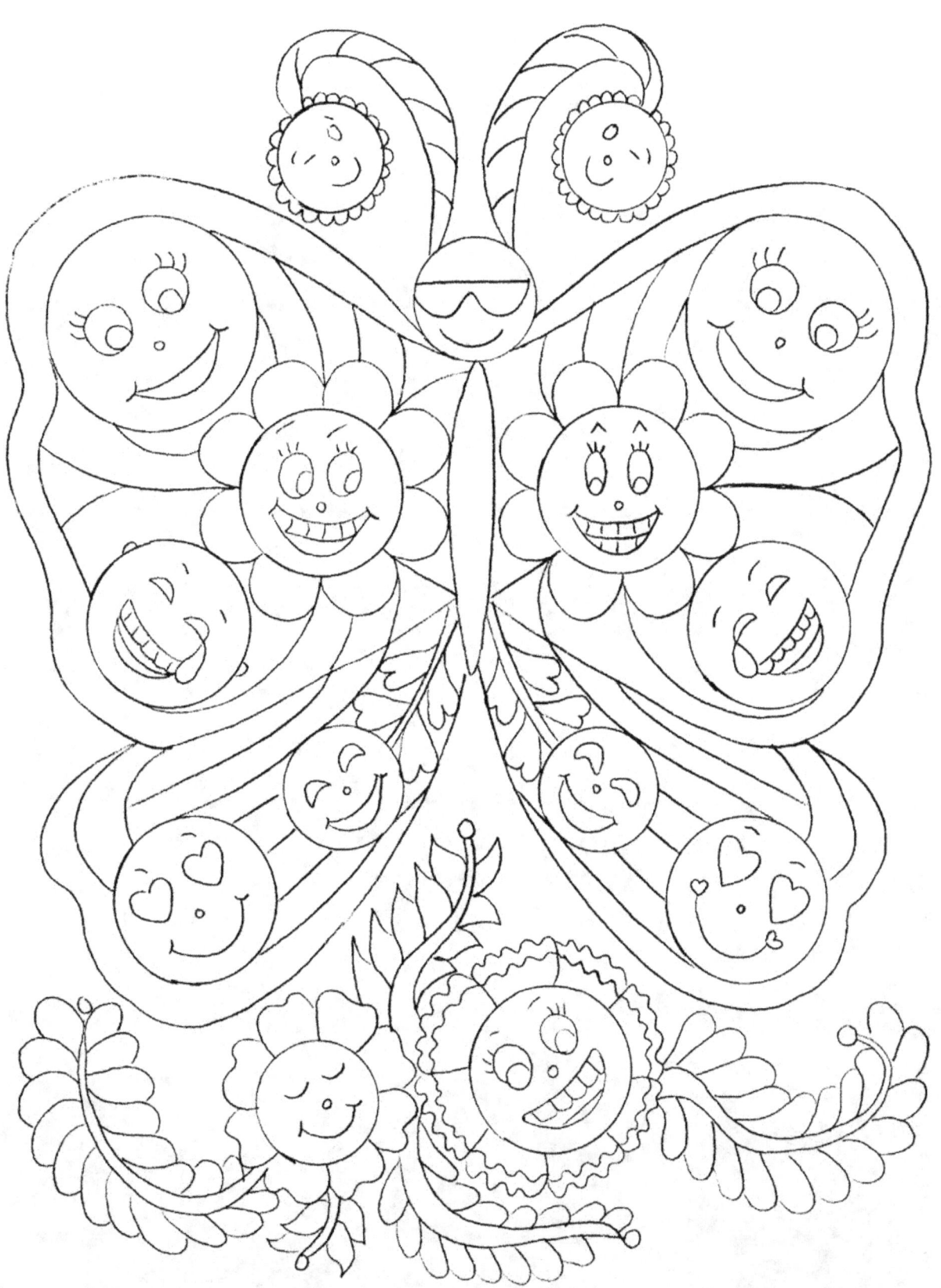

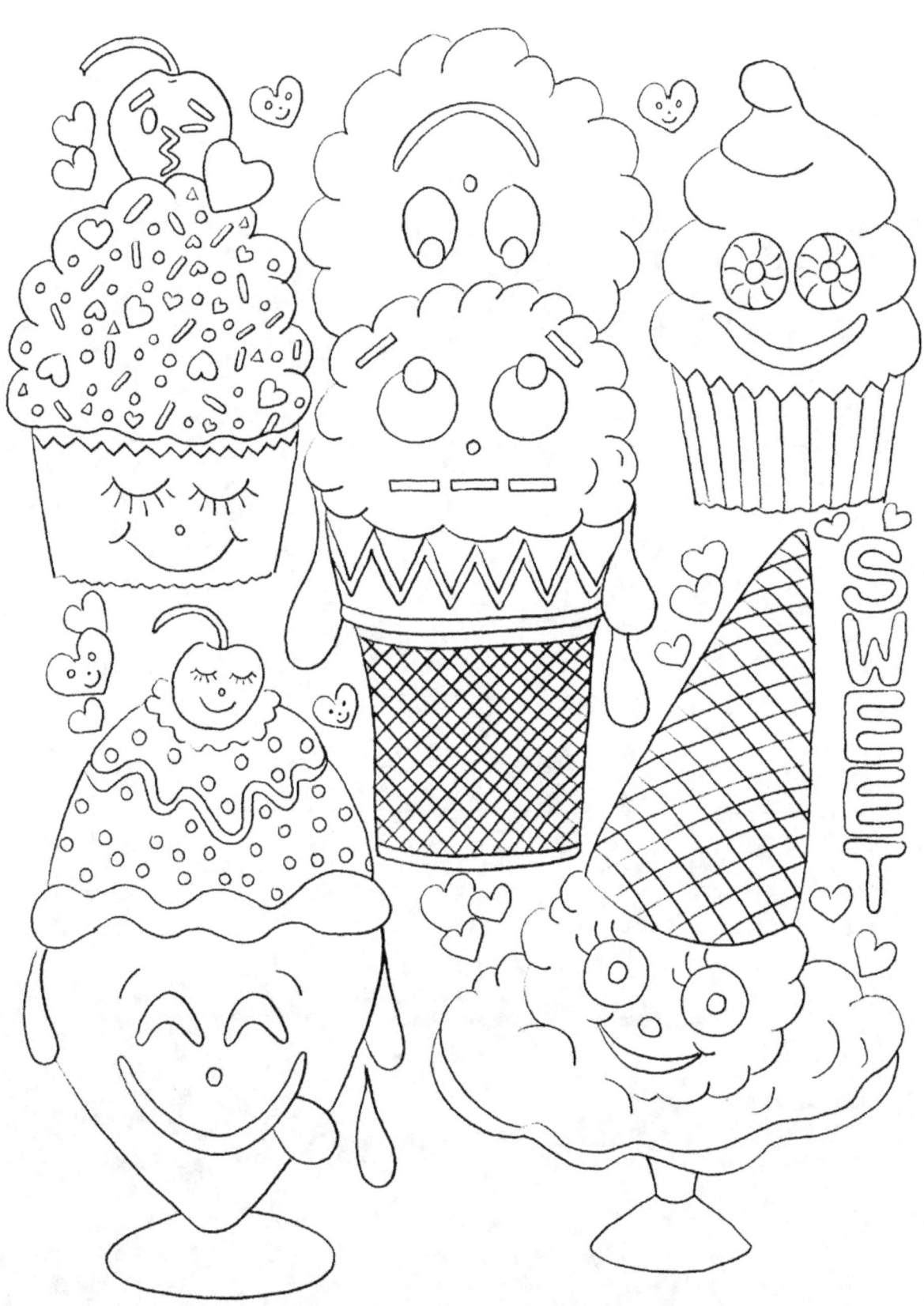

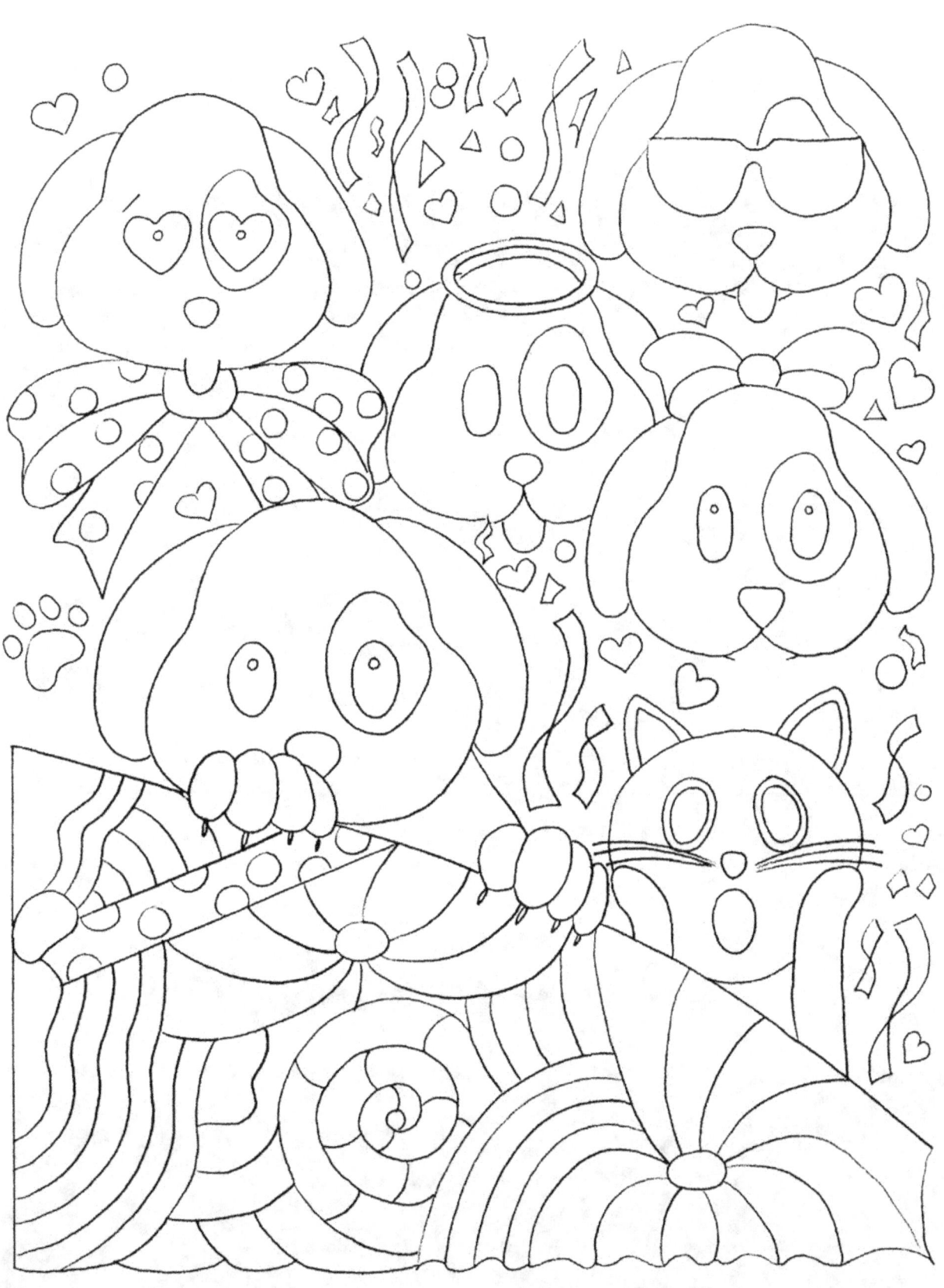

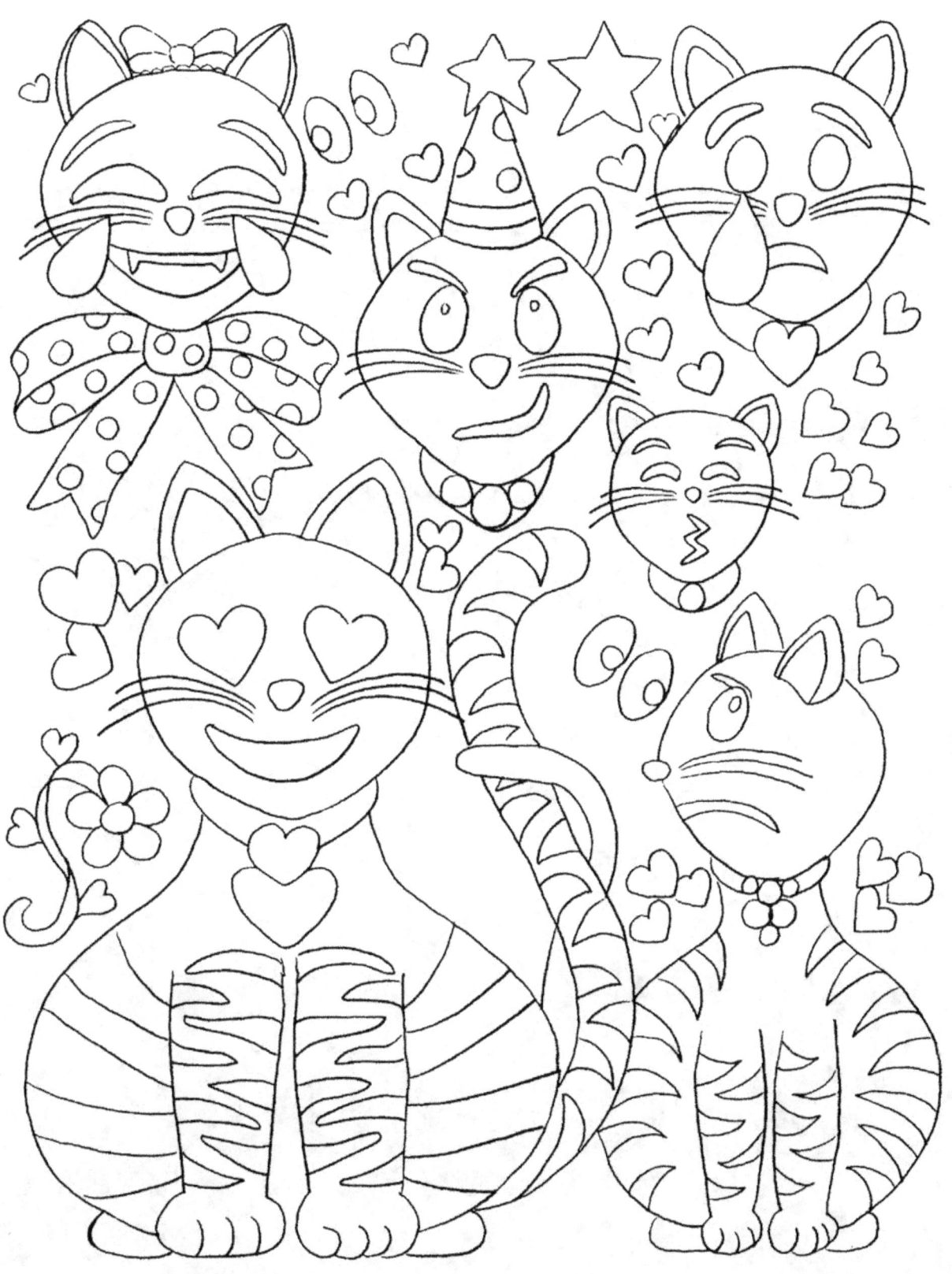

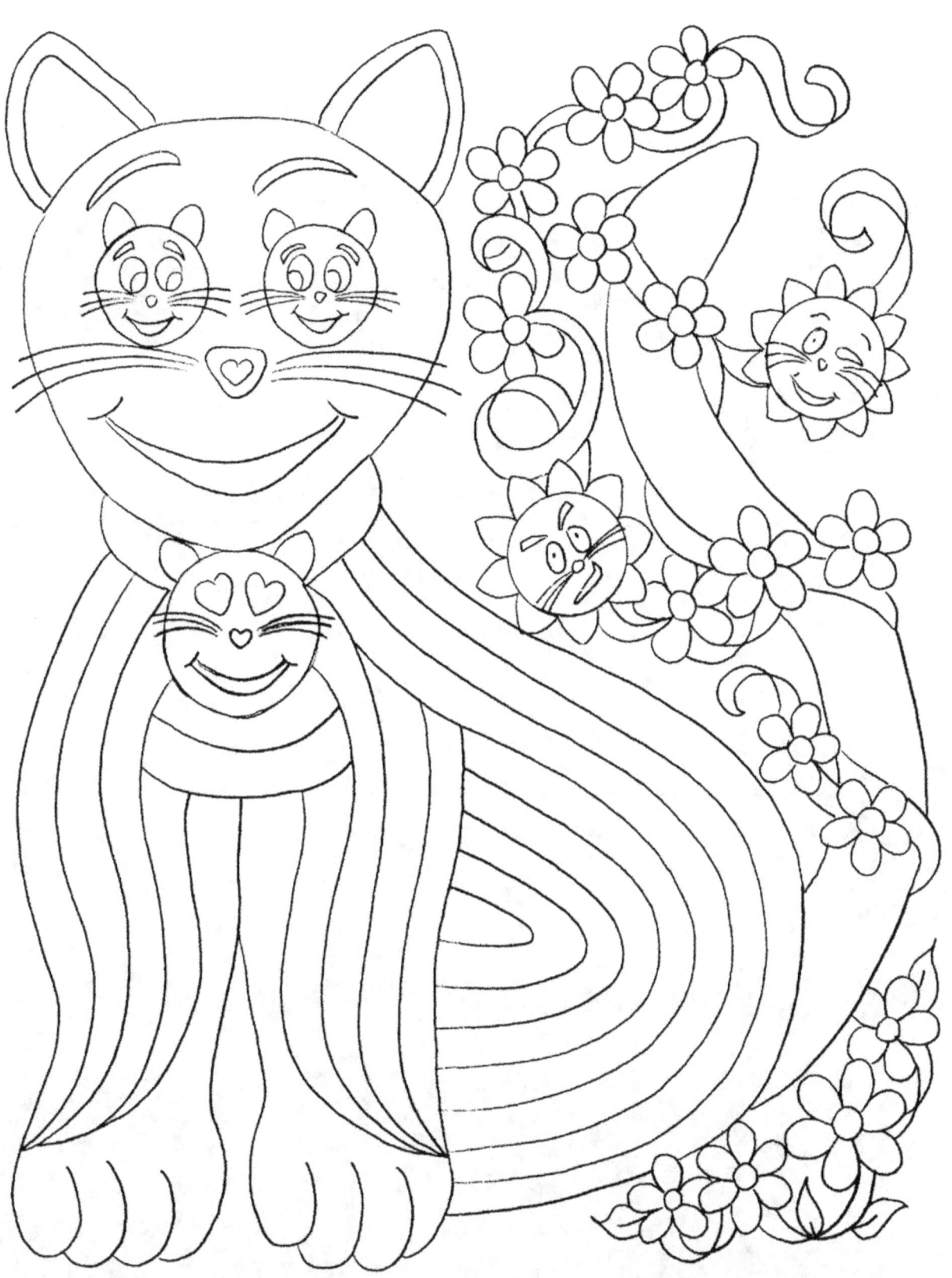

On the blank face, draw and color
an emoji that best describes you.

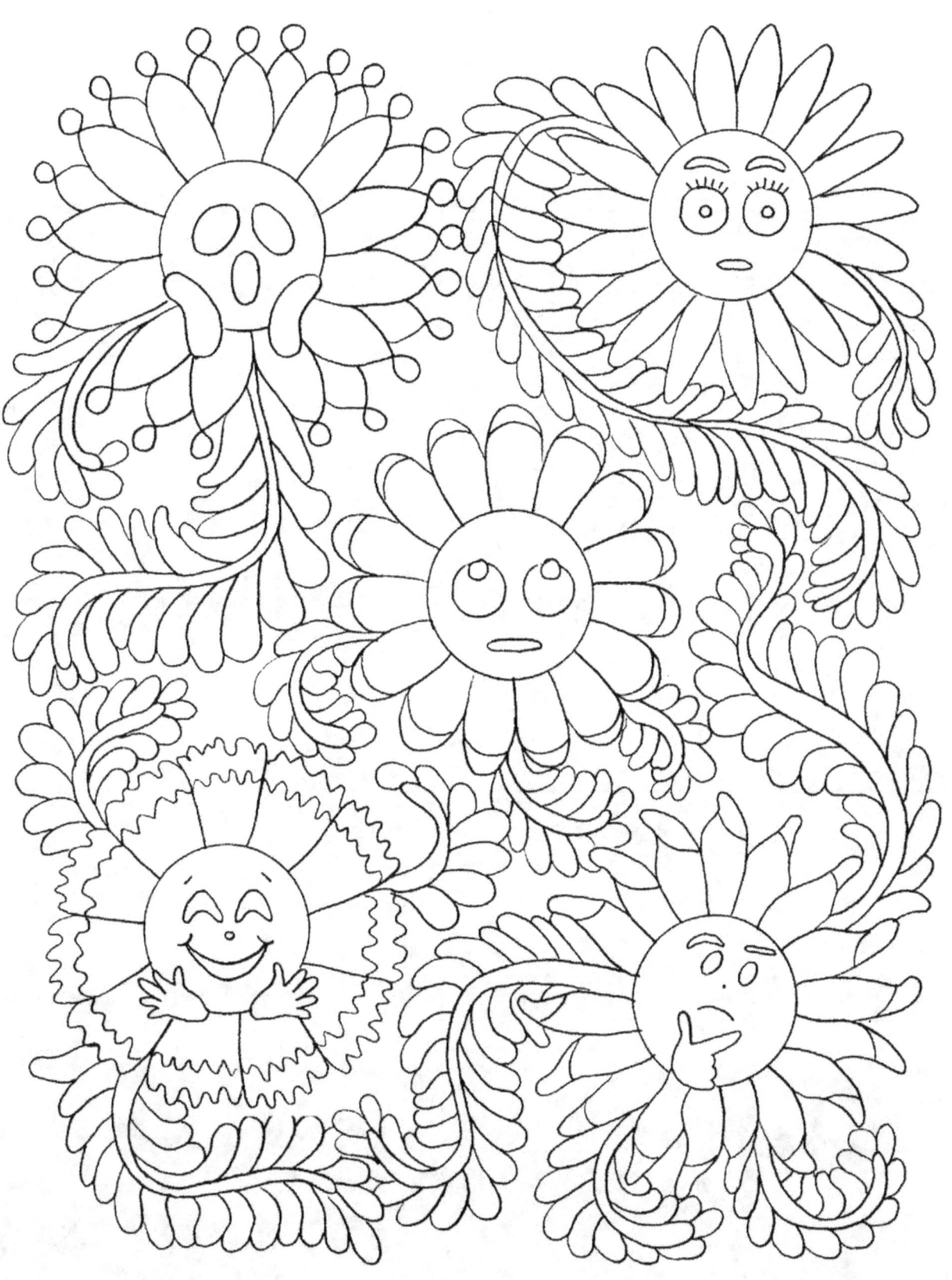

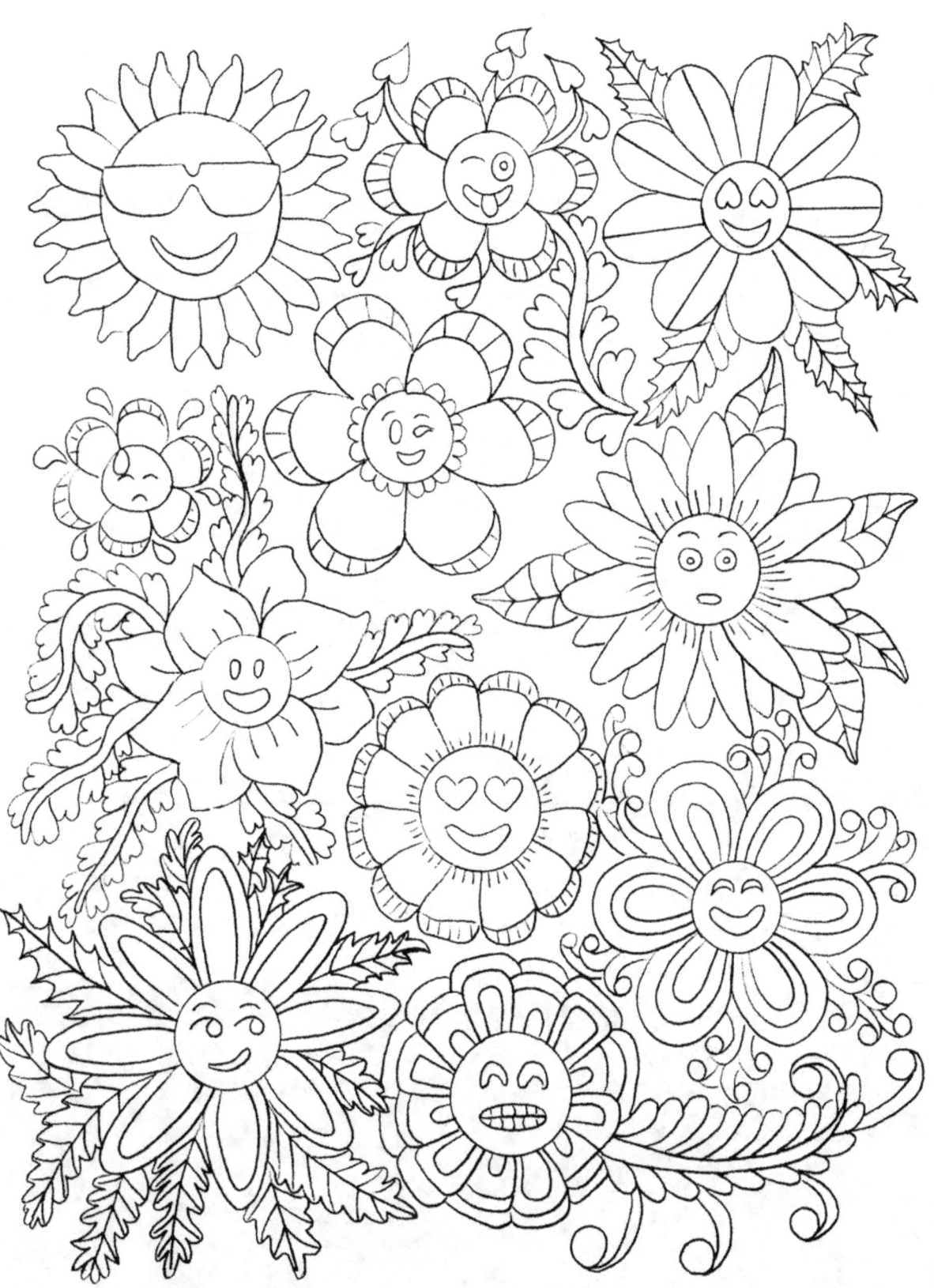

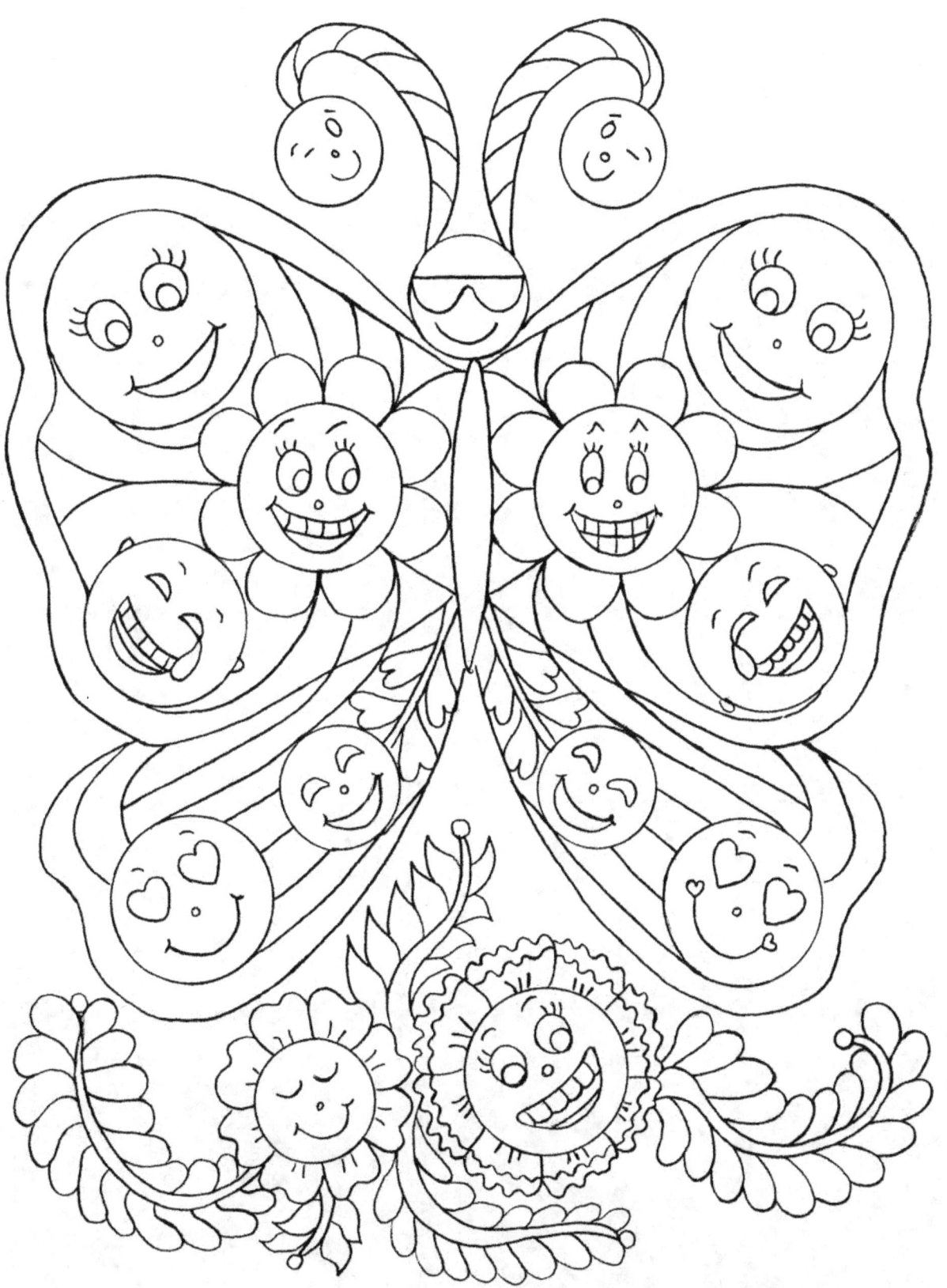

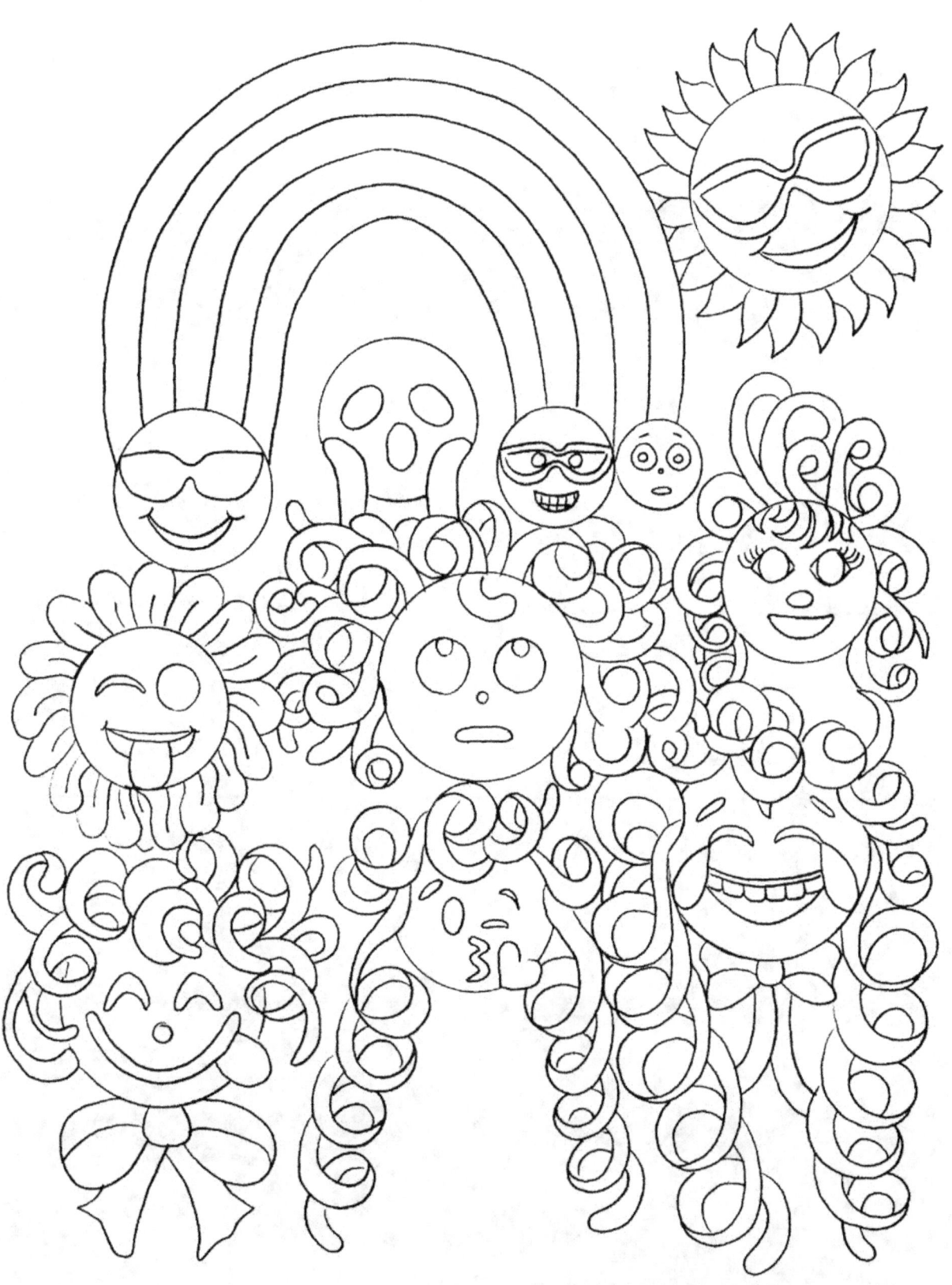

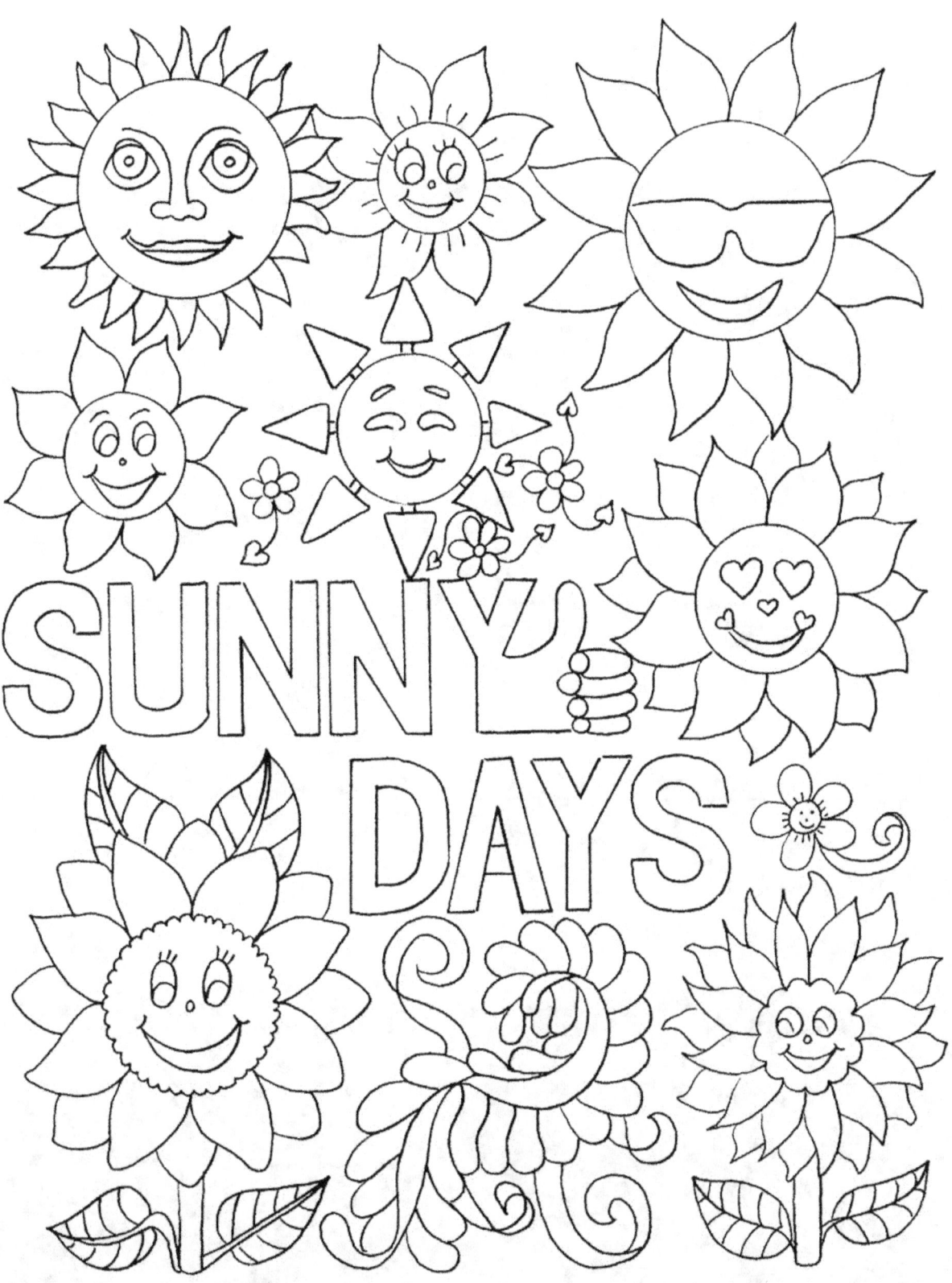

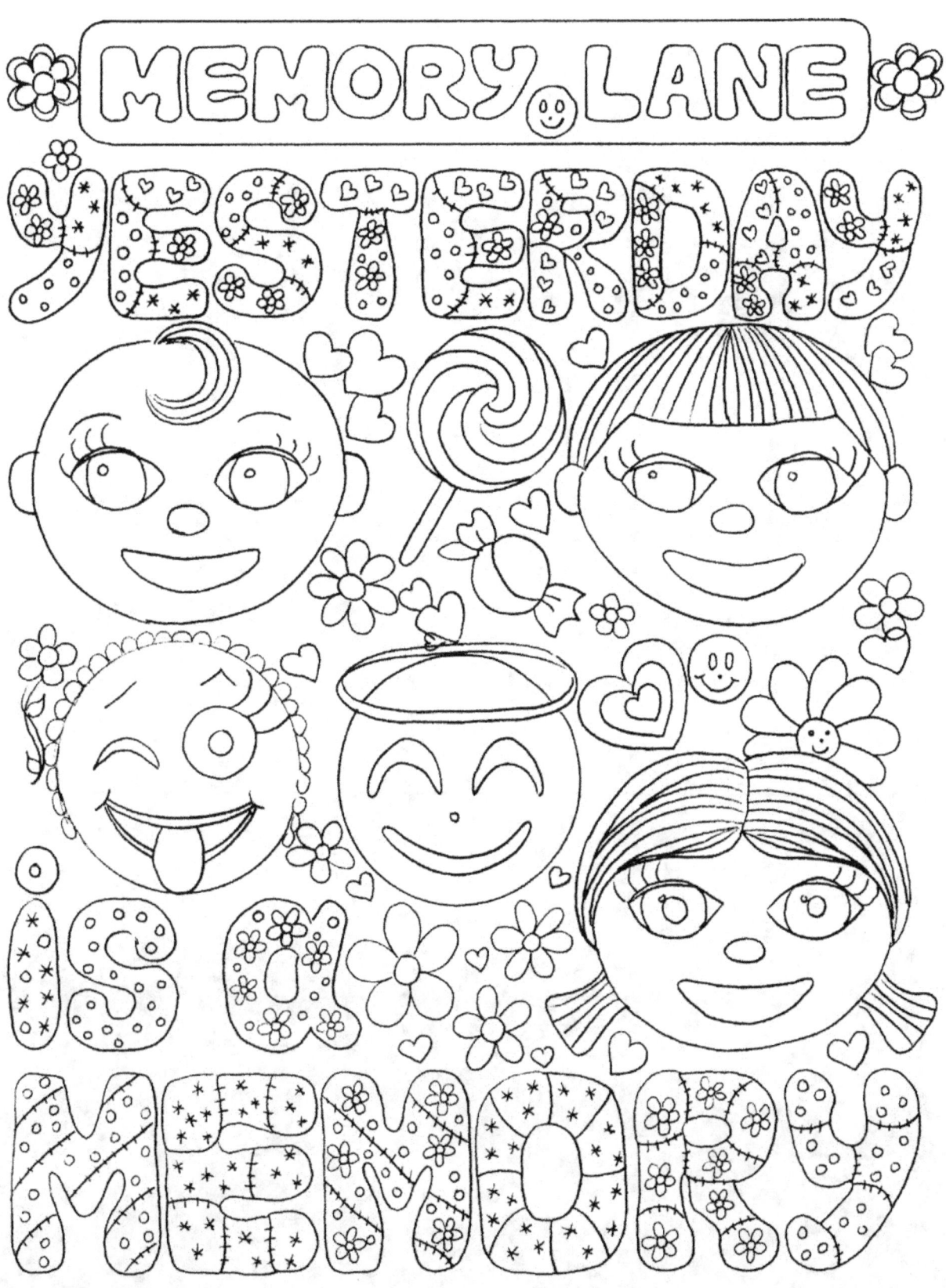

MEMORY LANE

YESTERDAY IS A MEMORY

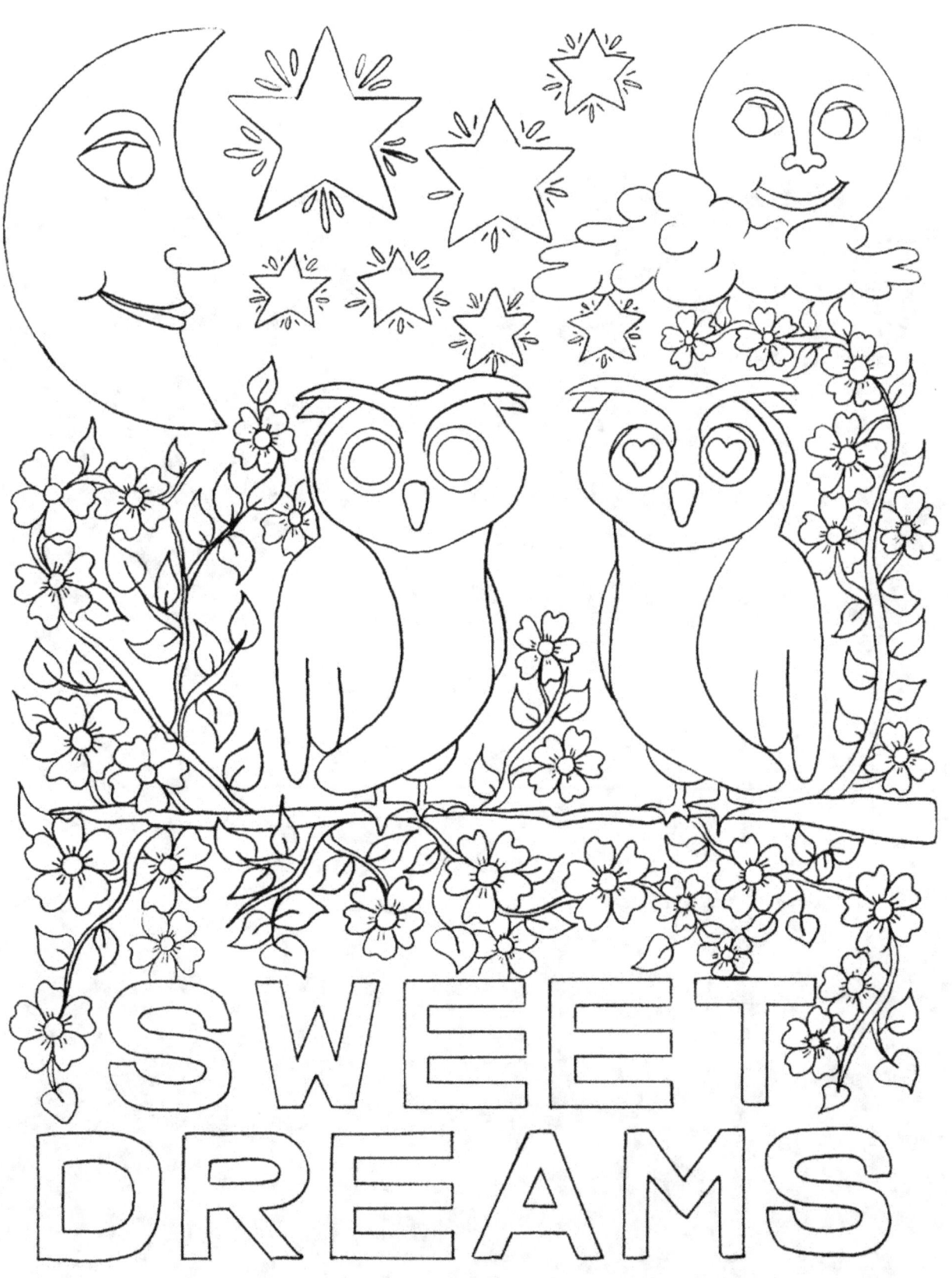

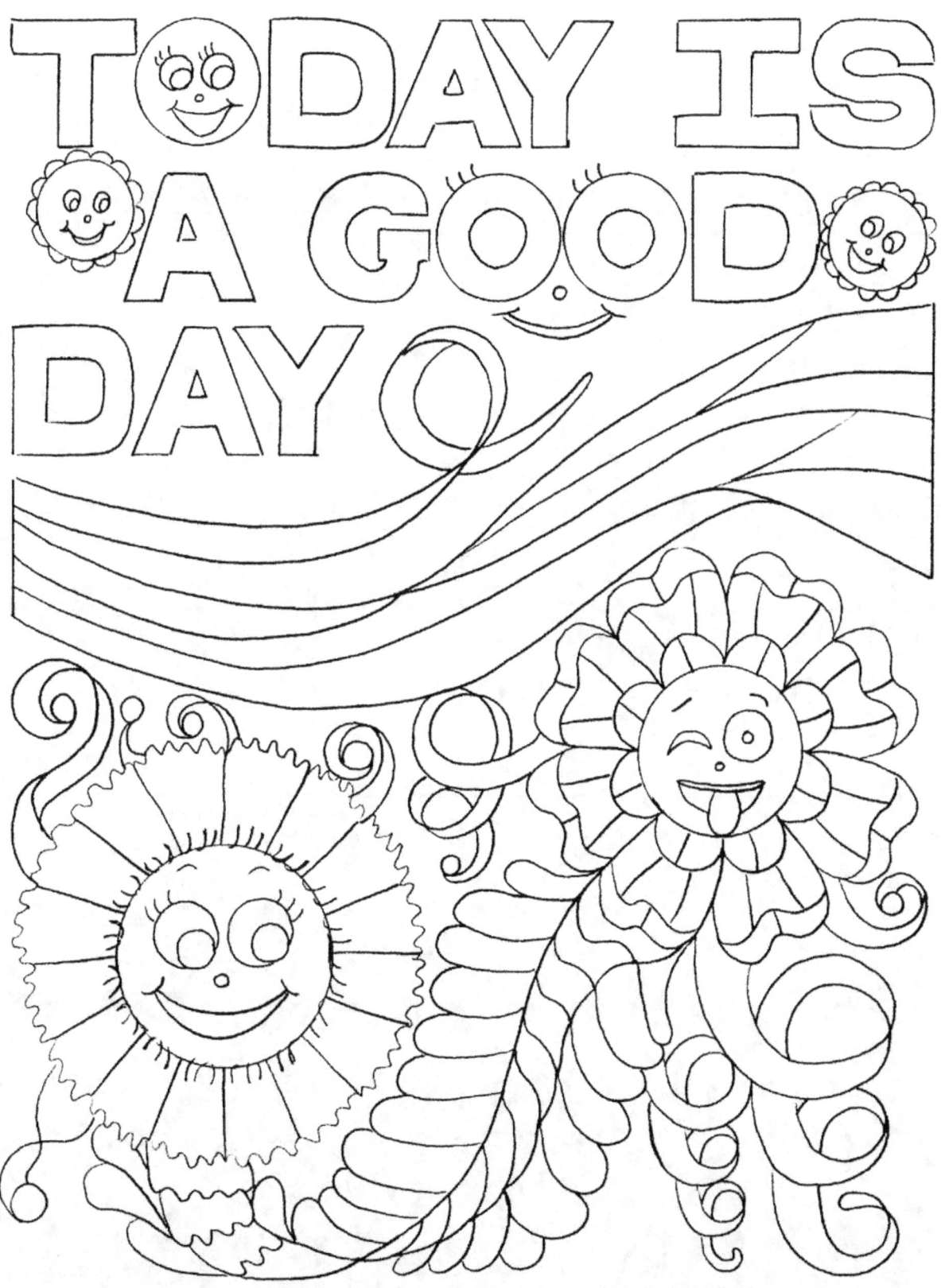

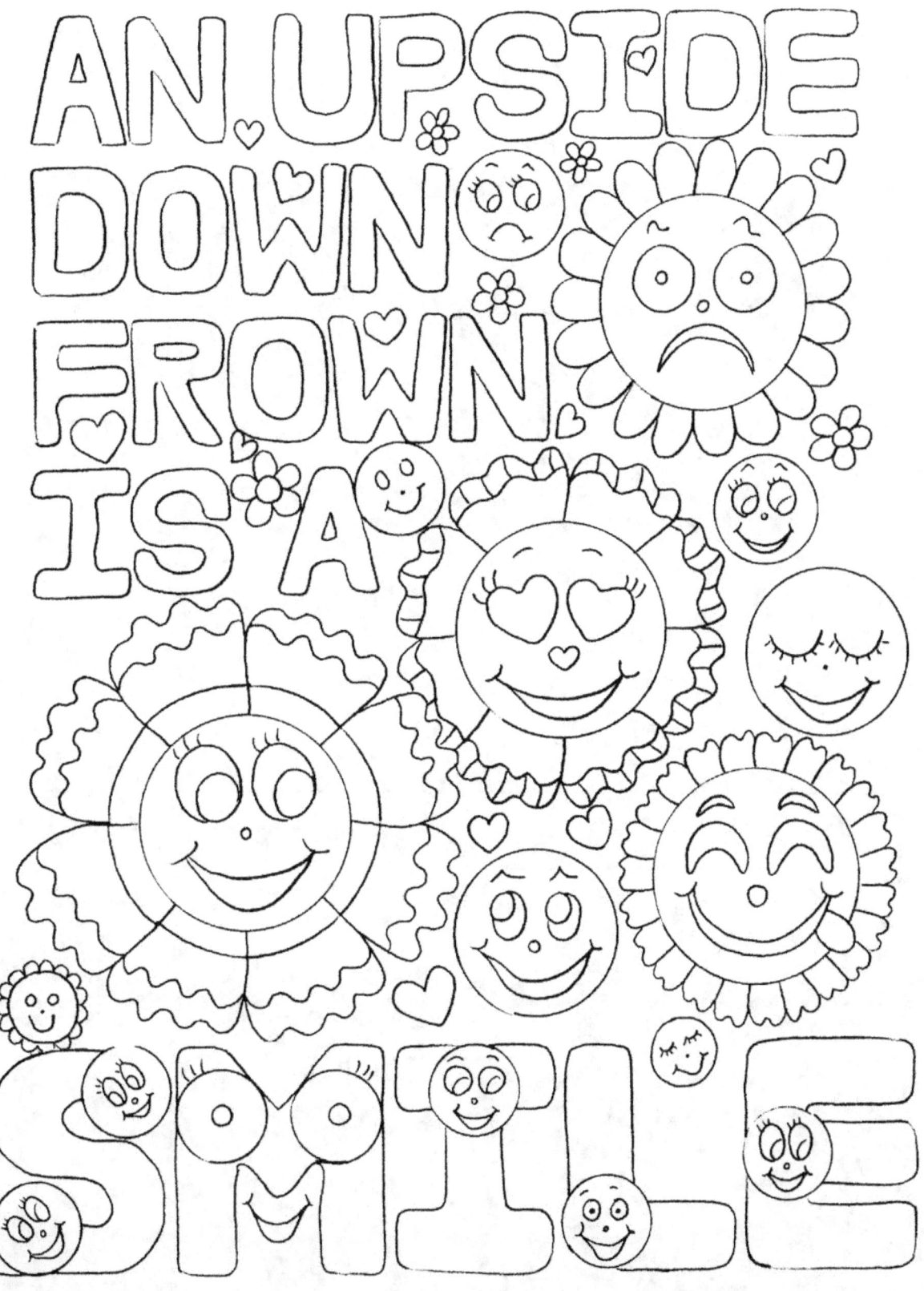

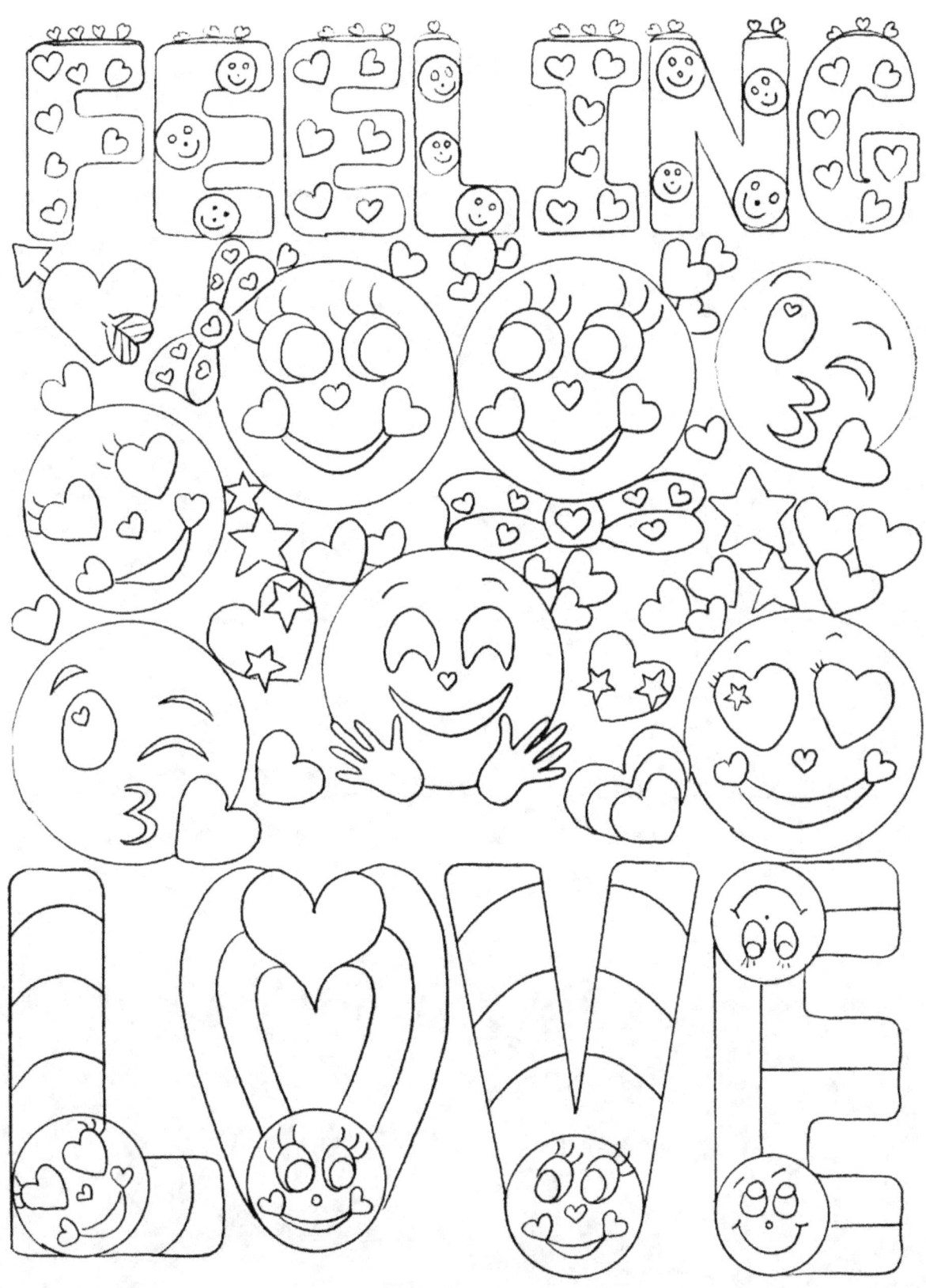

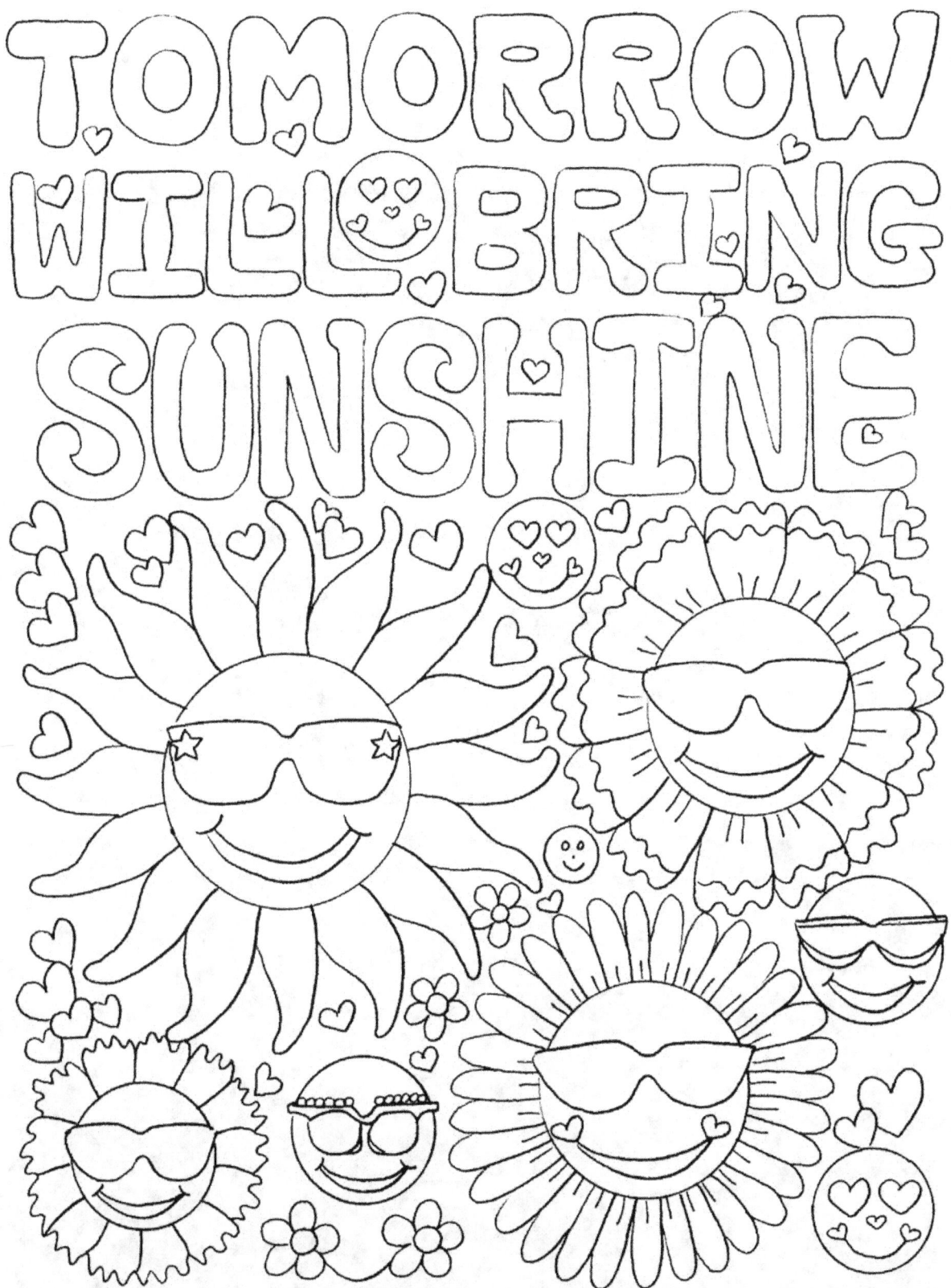

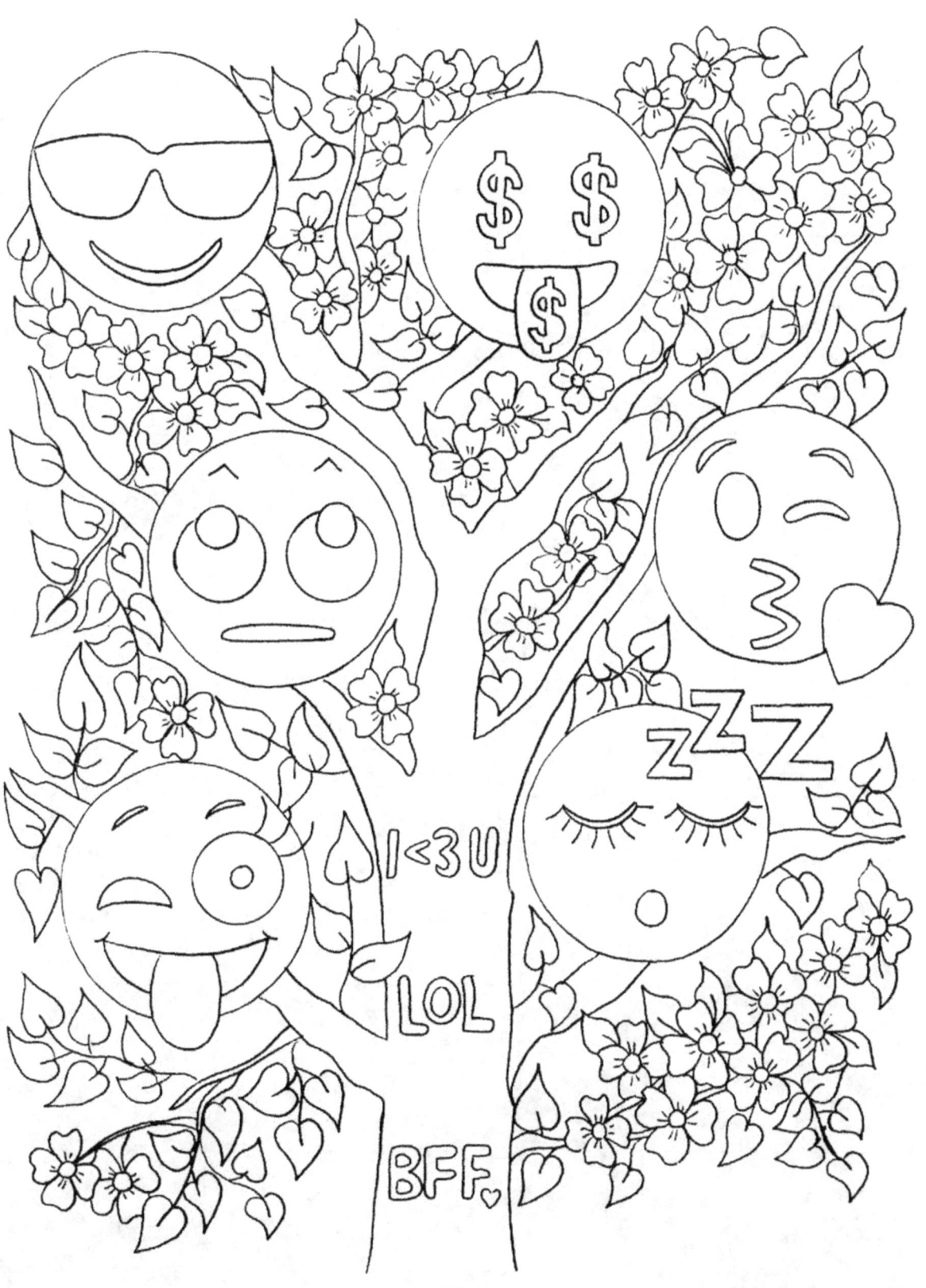

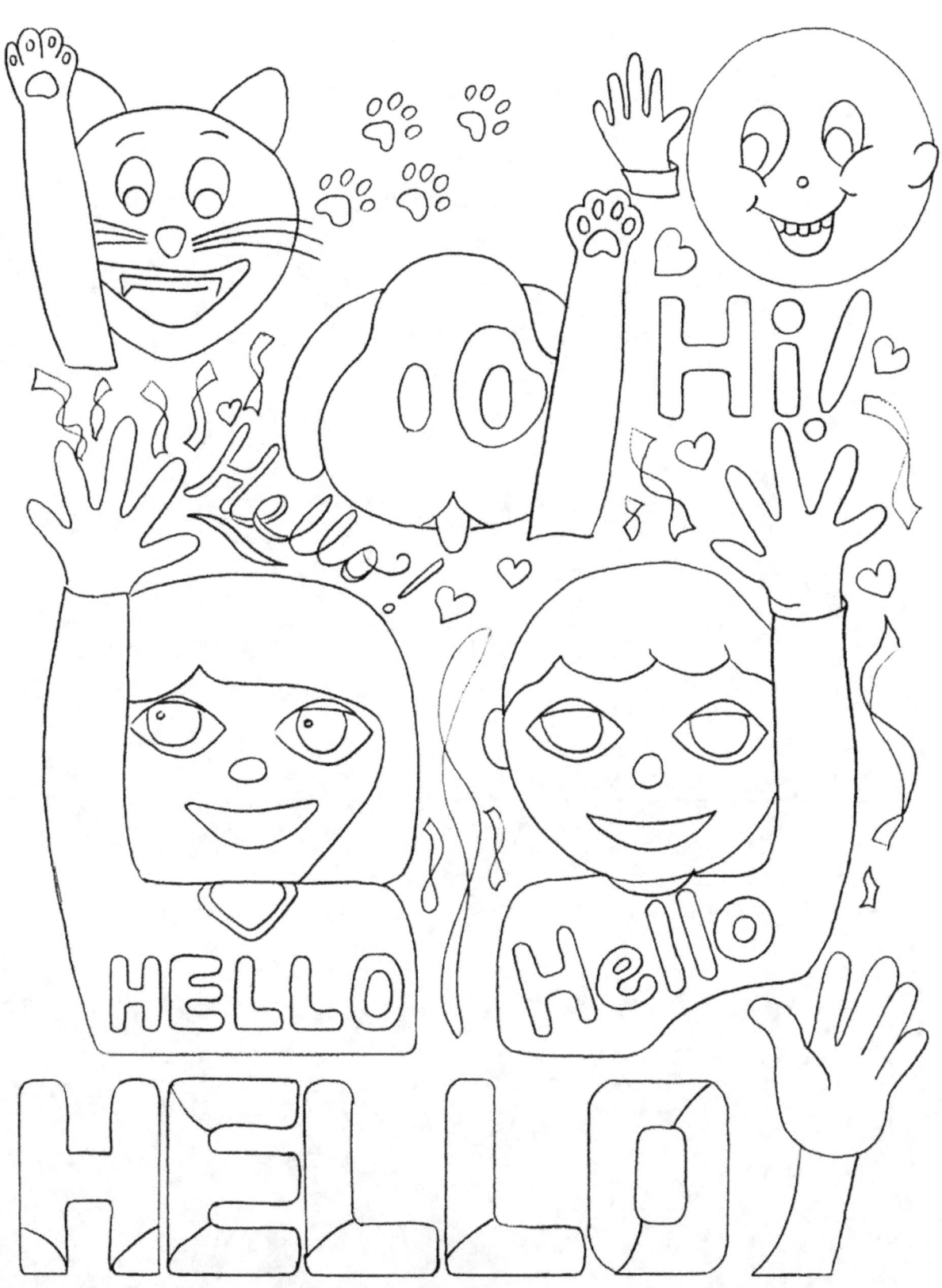

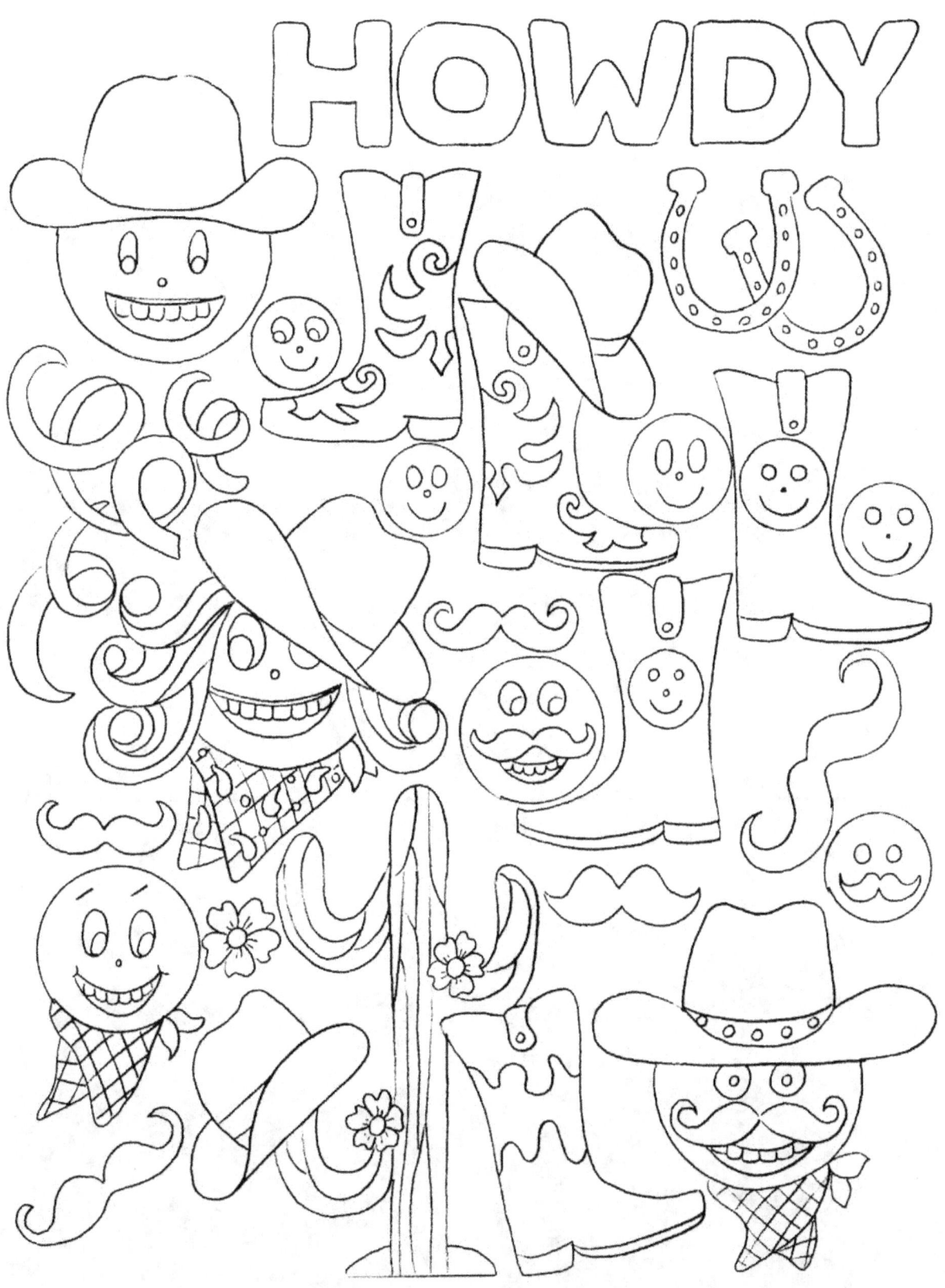

WHATEVER

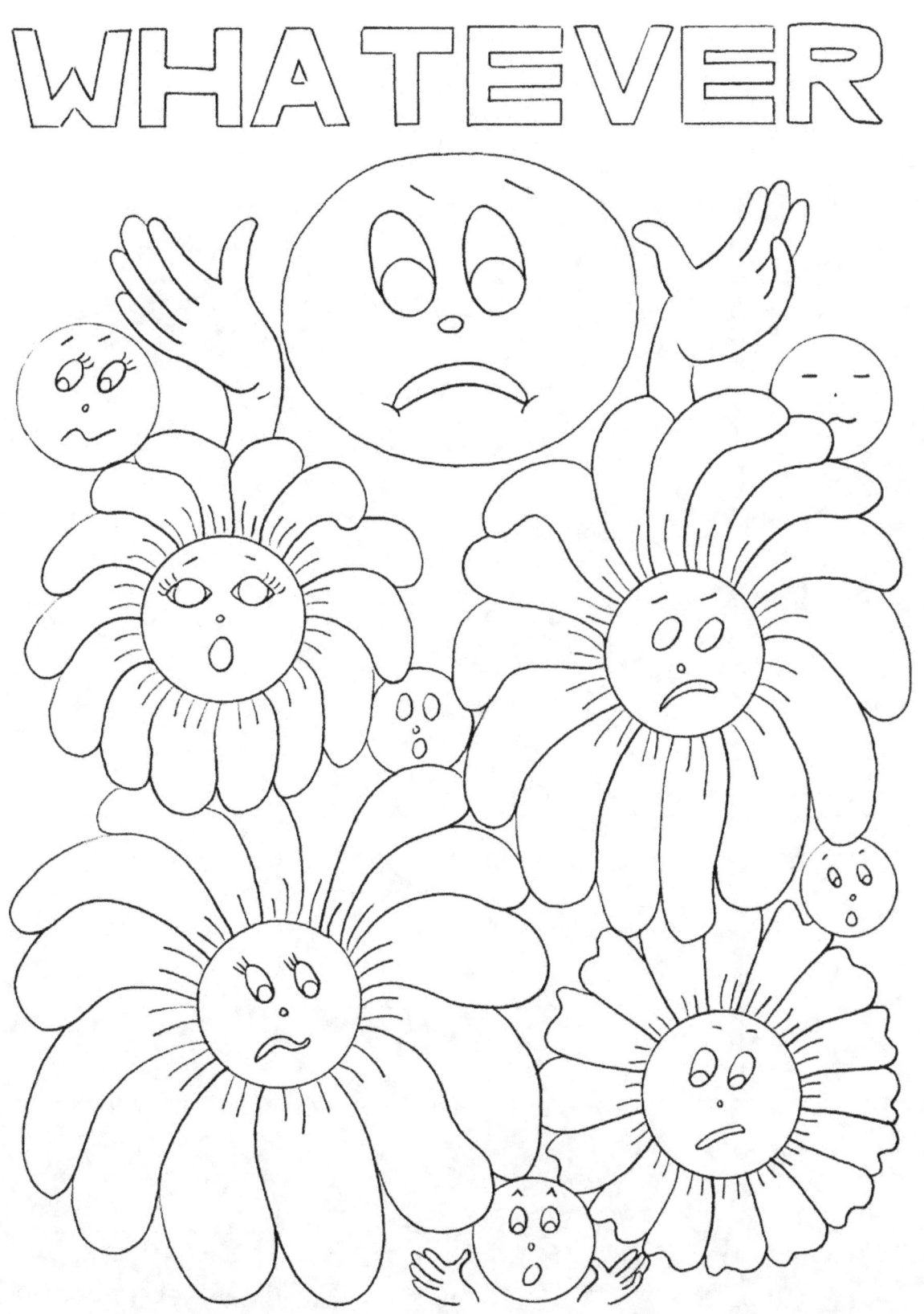

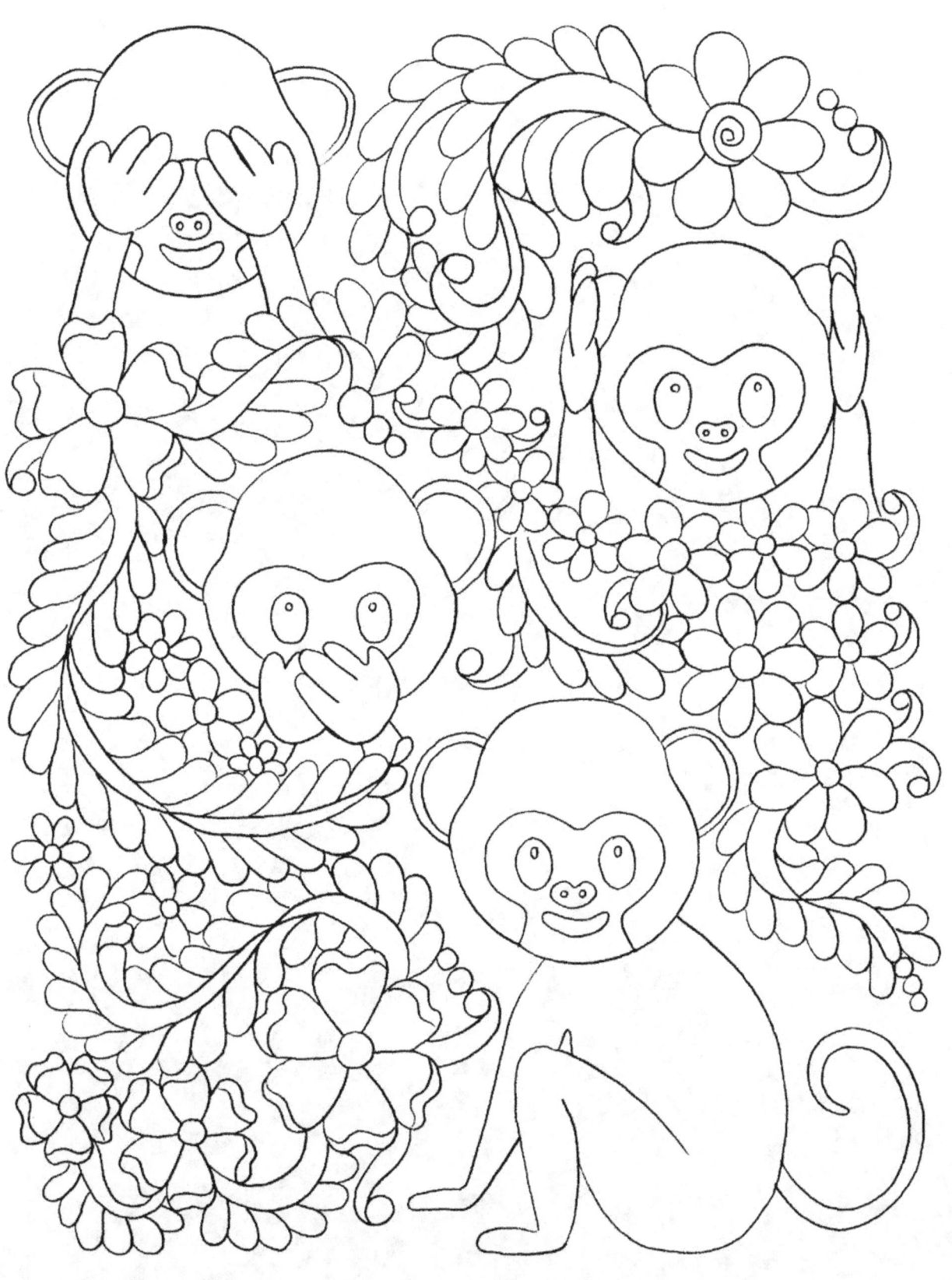

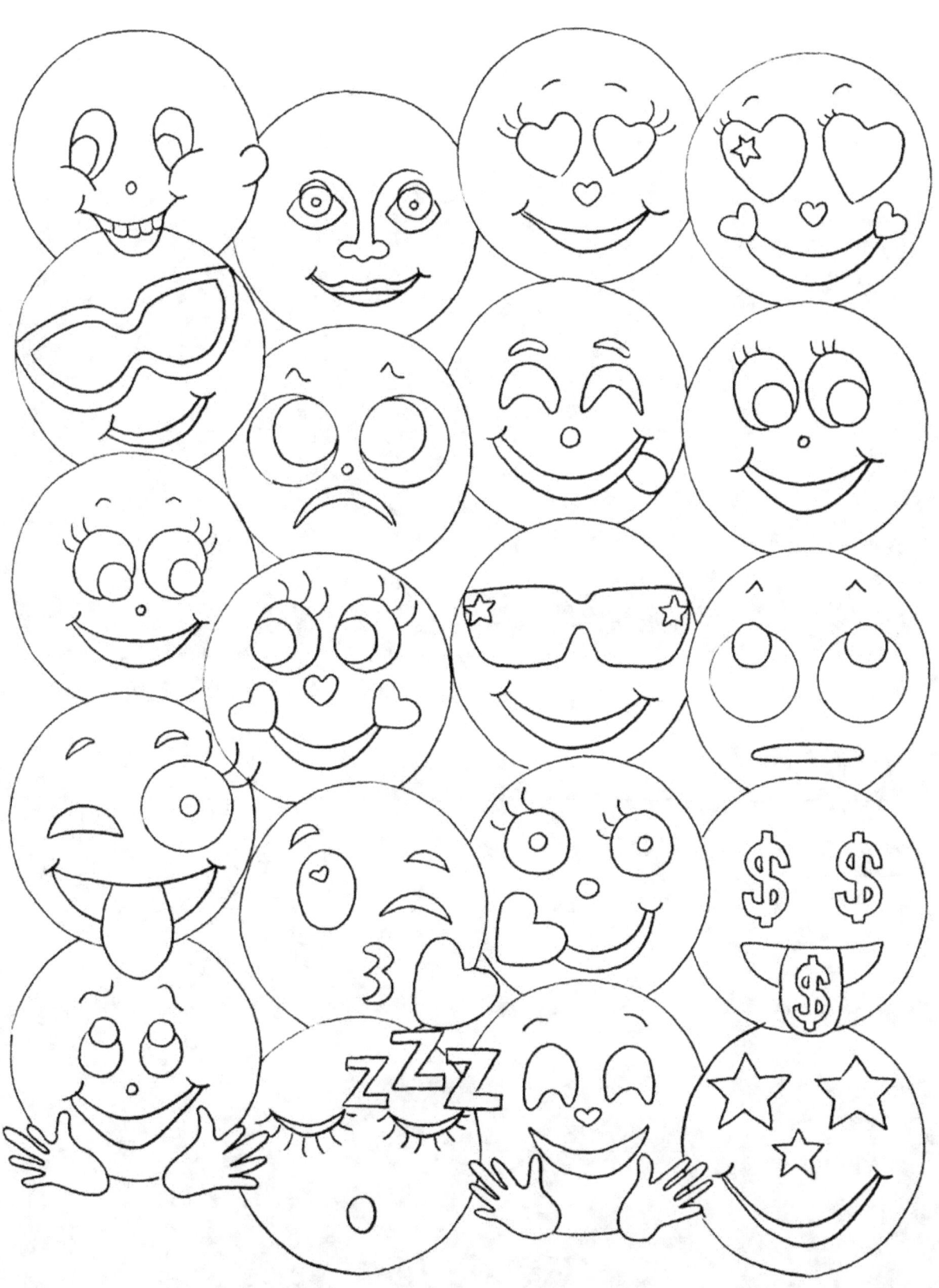

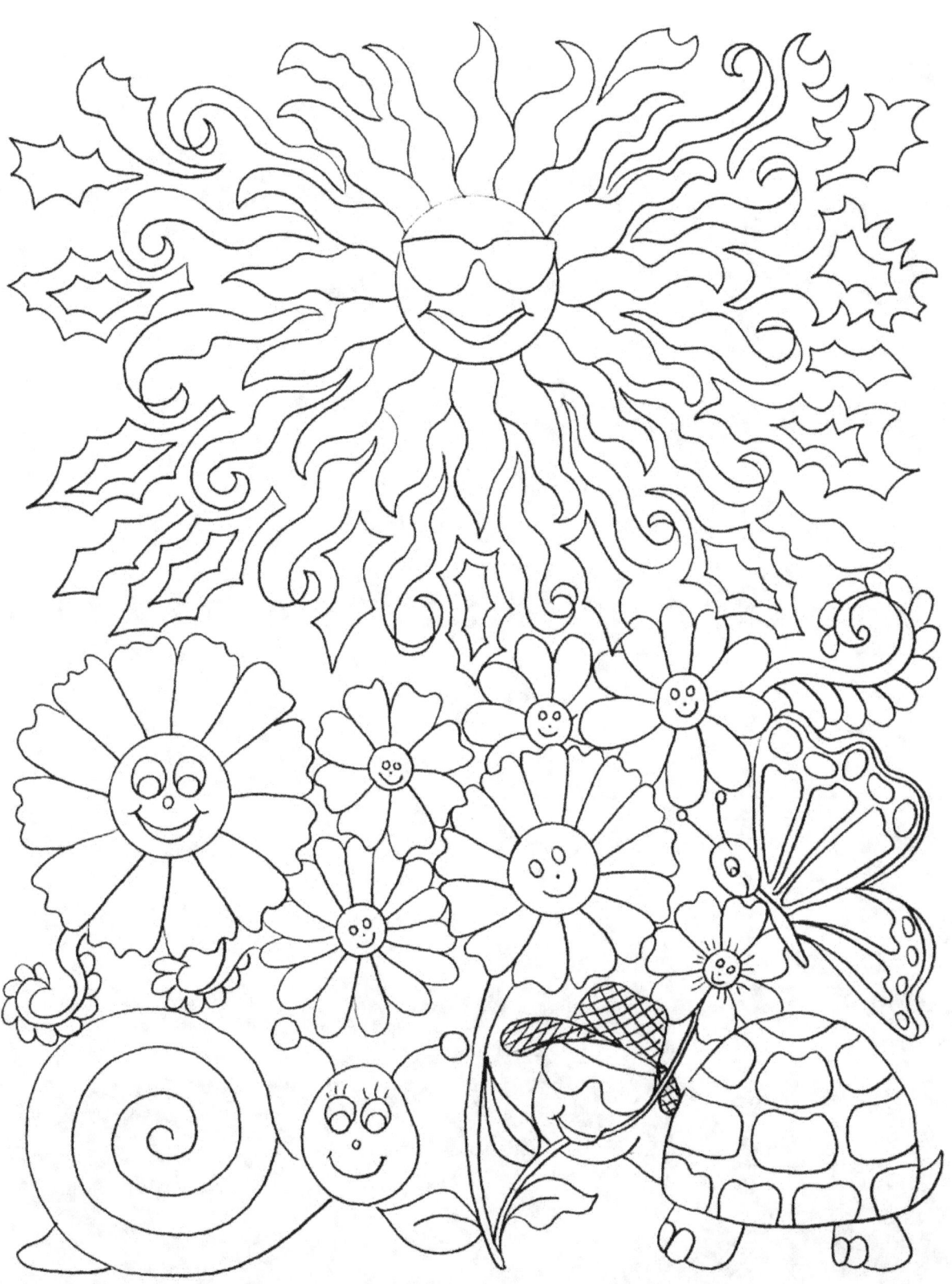

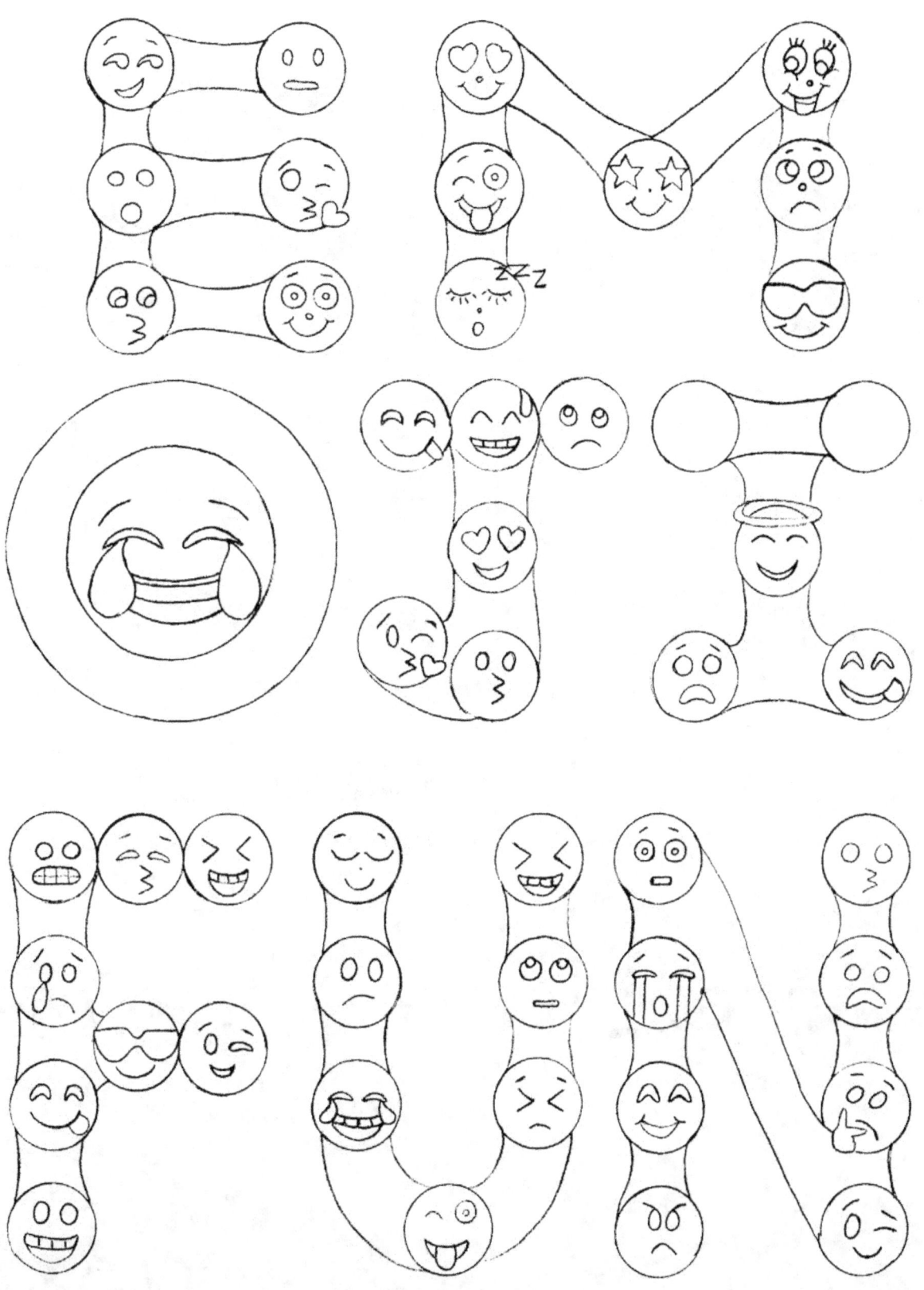

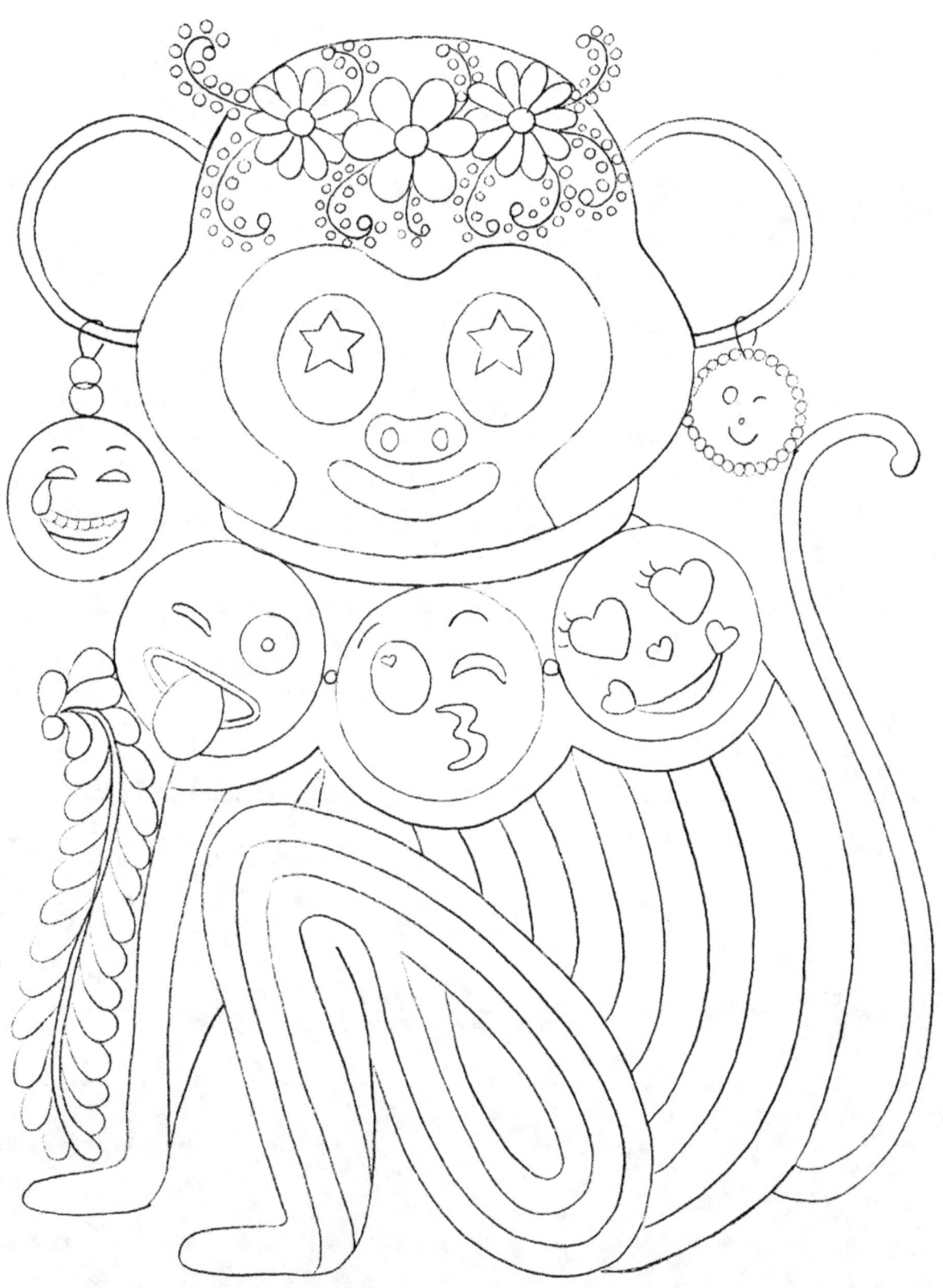

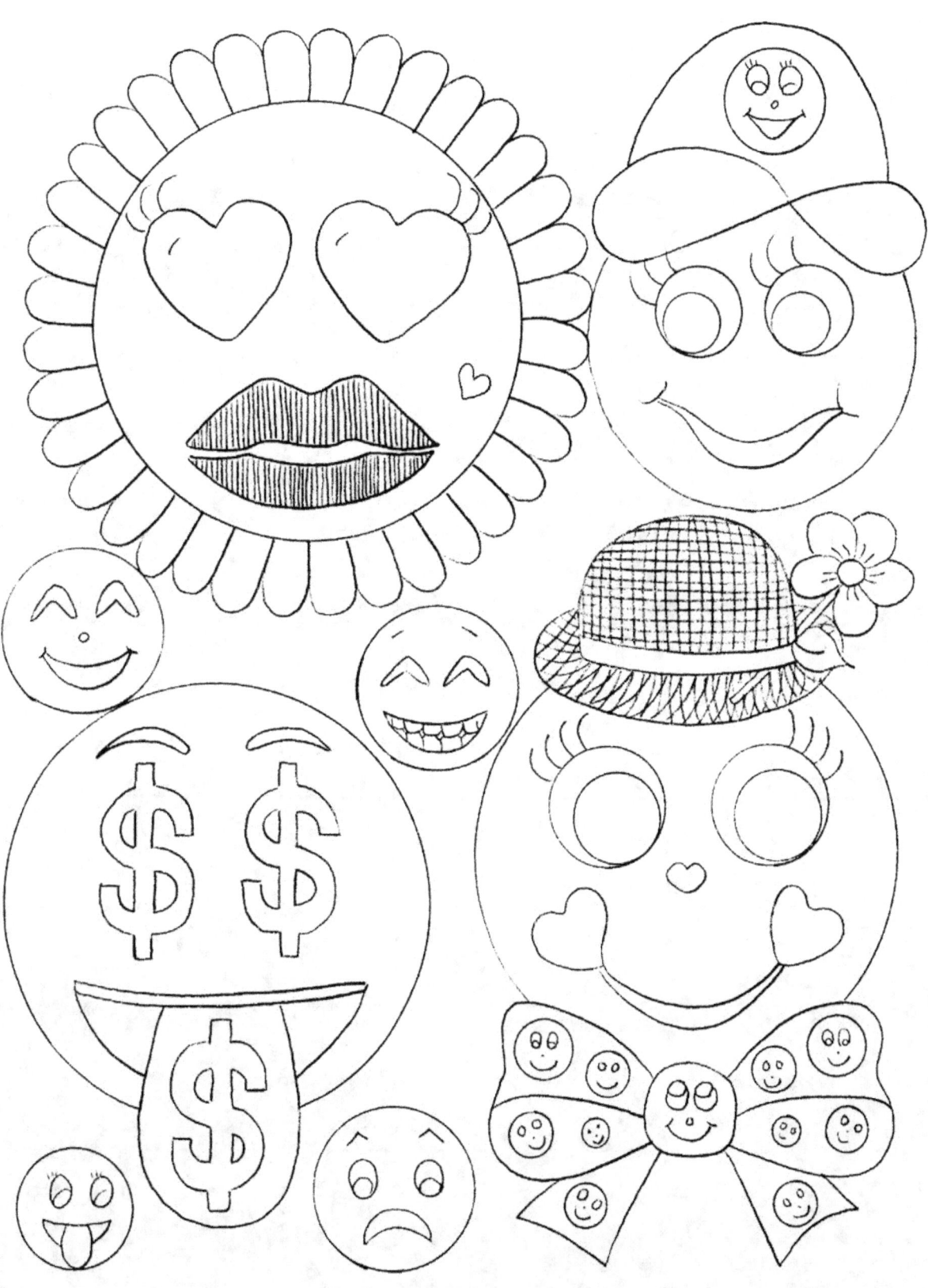

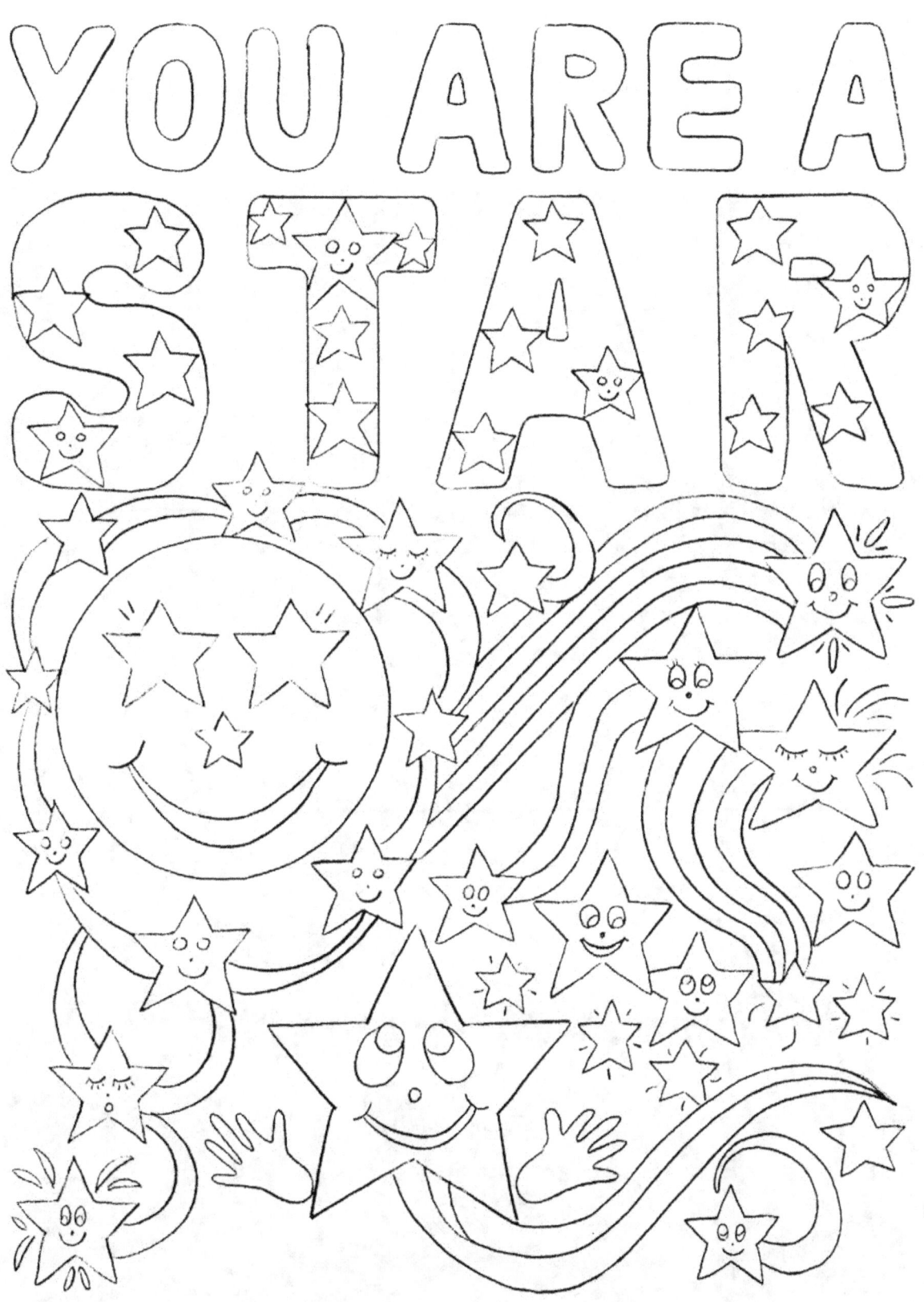

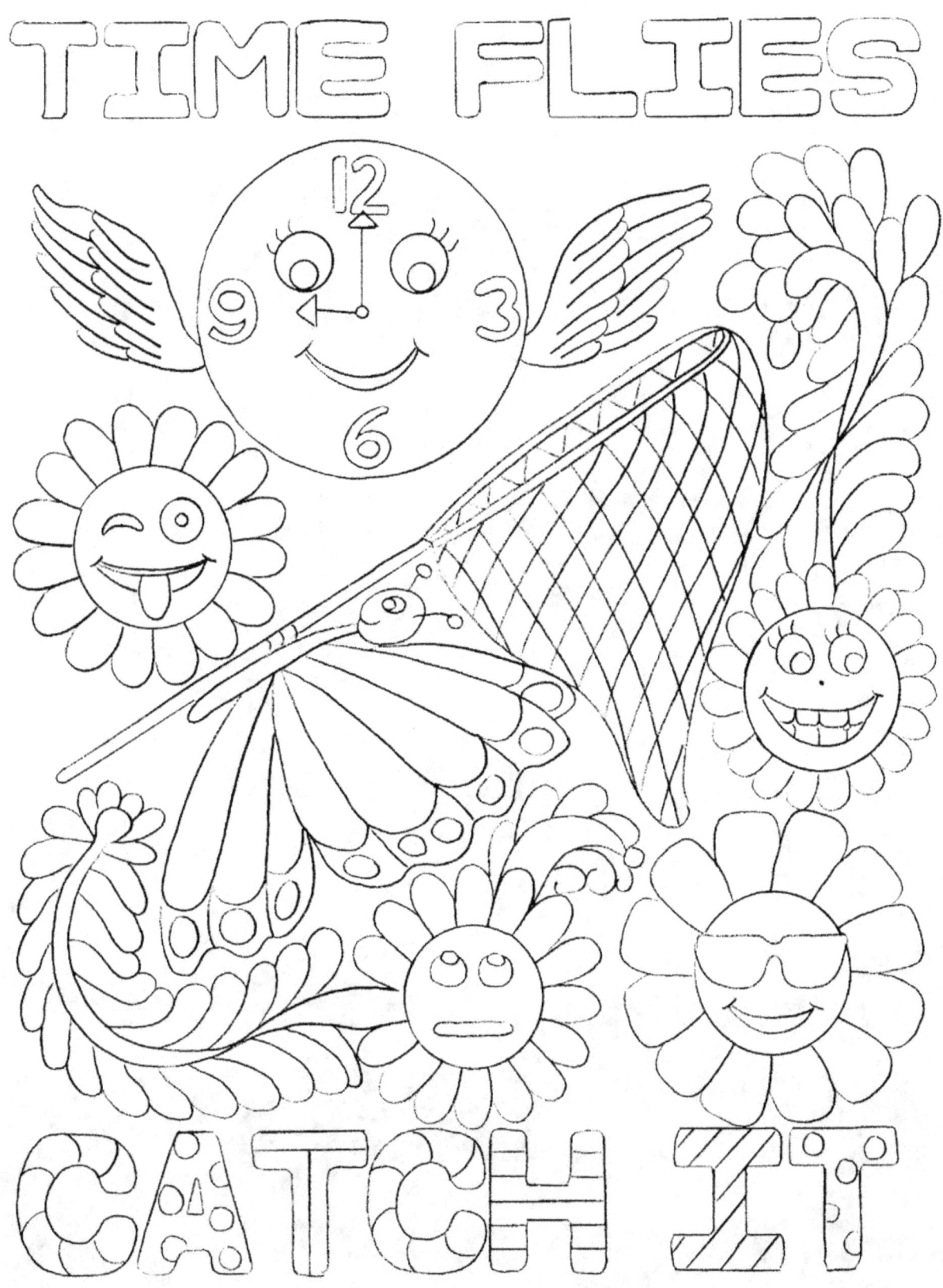

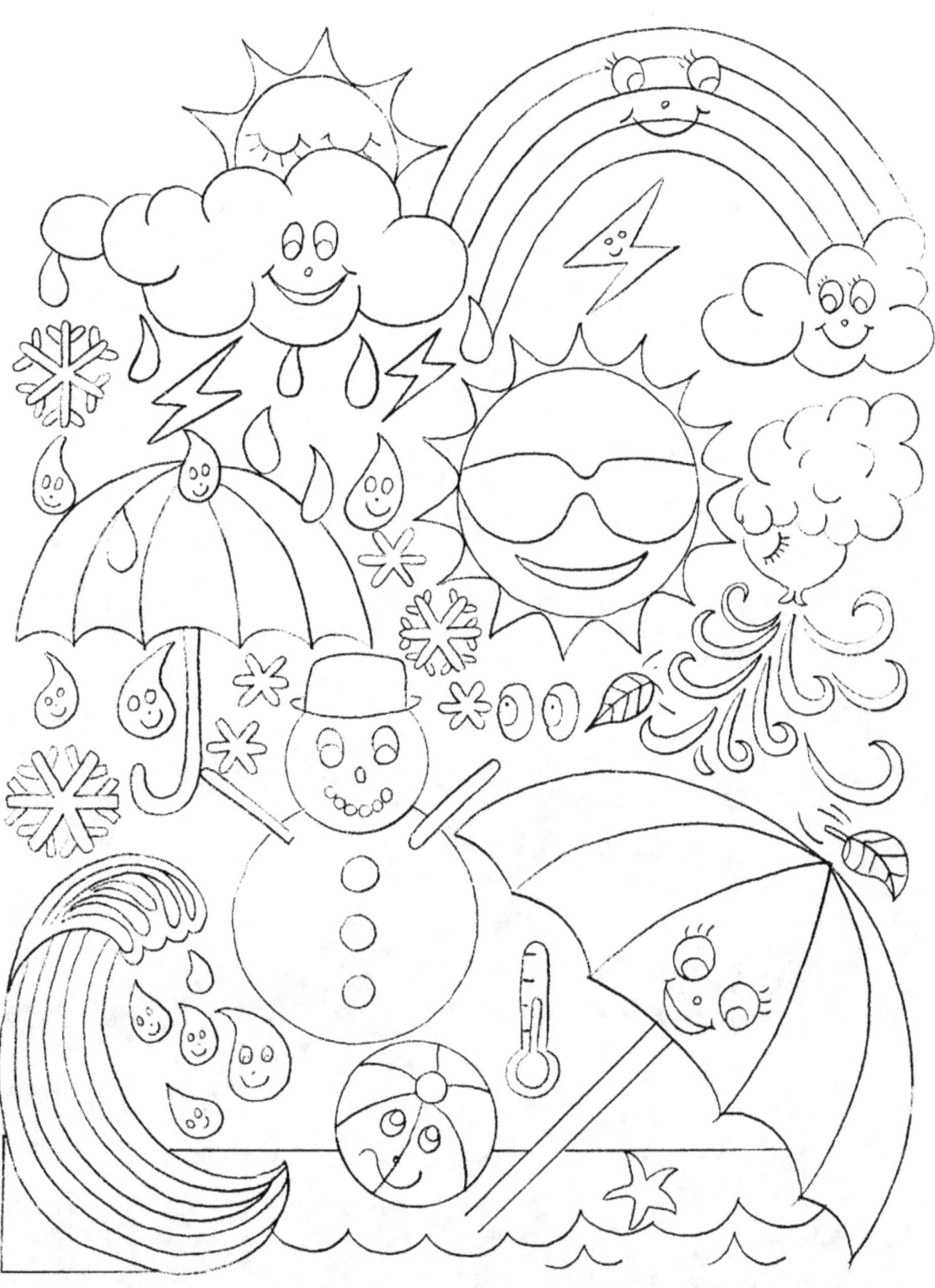

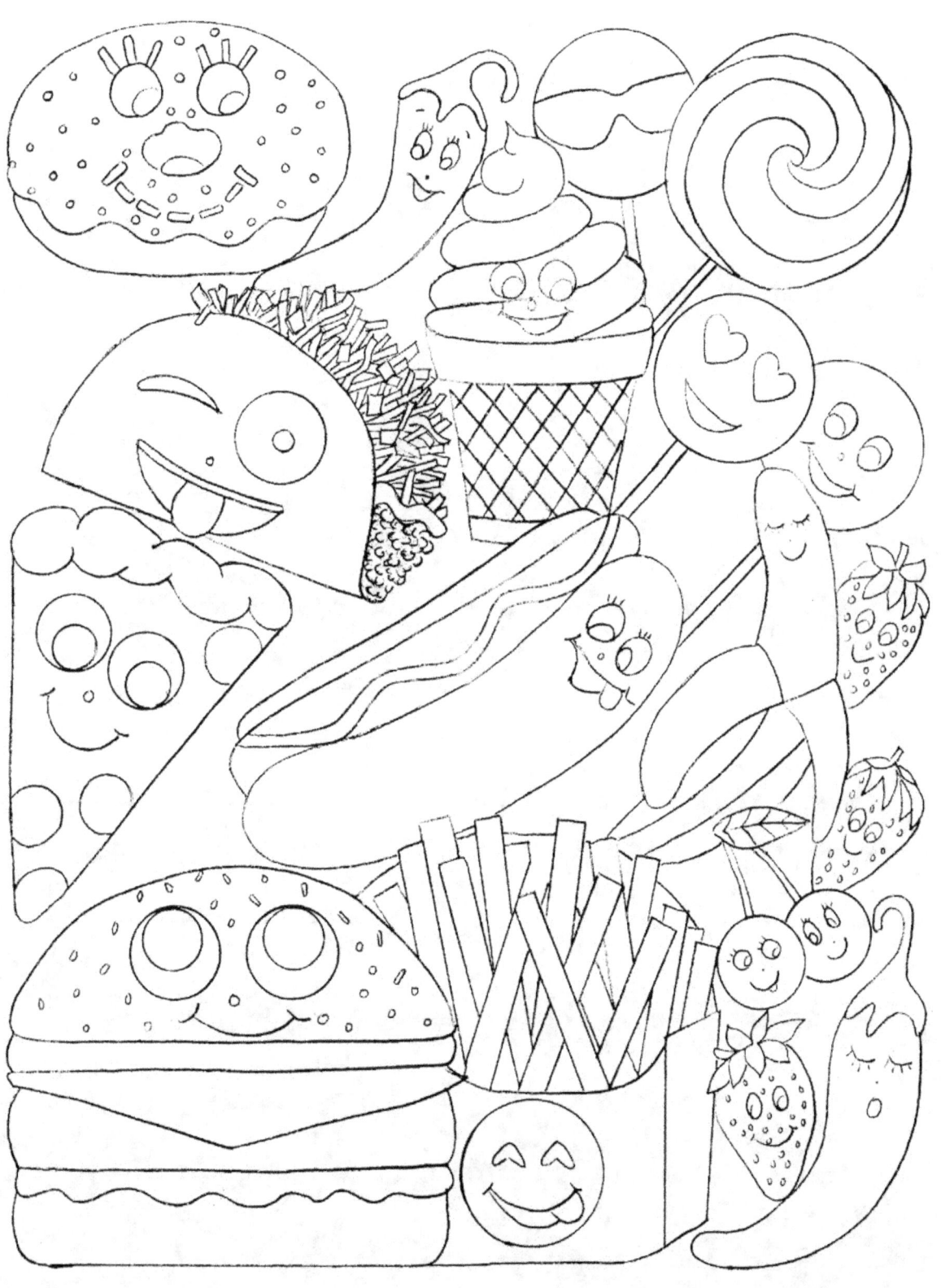

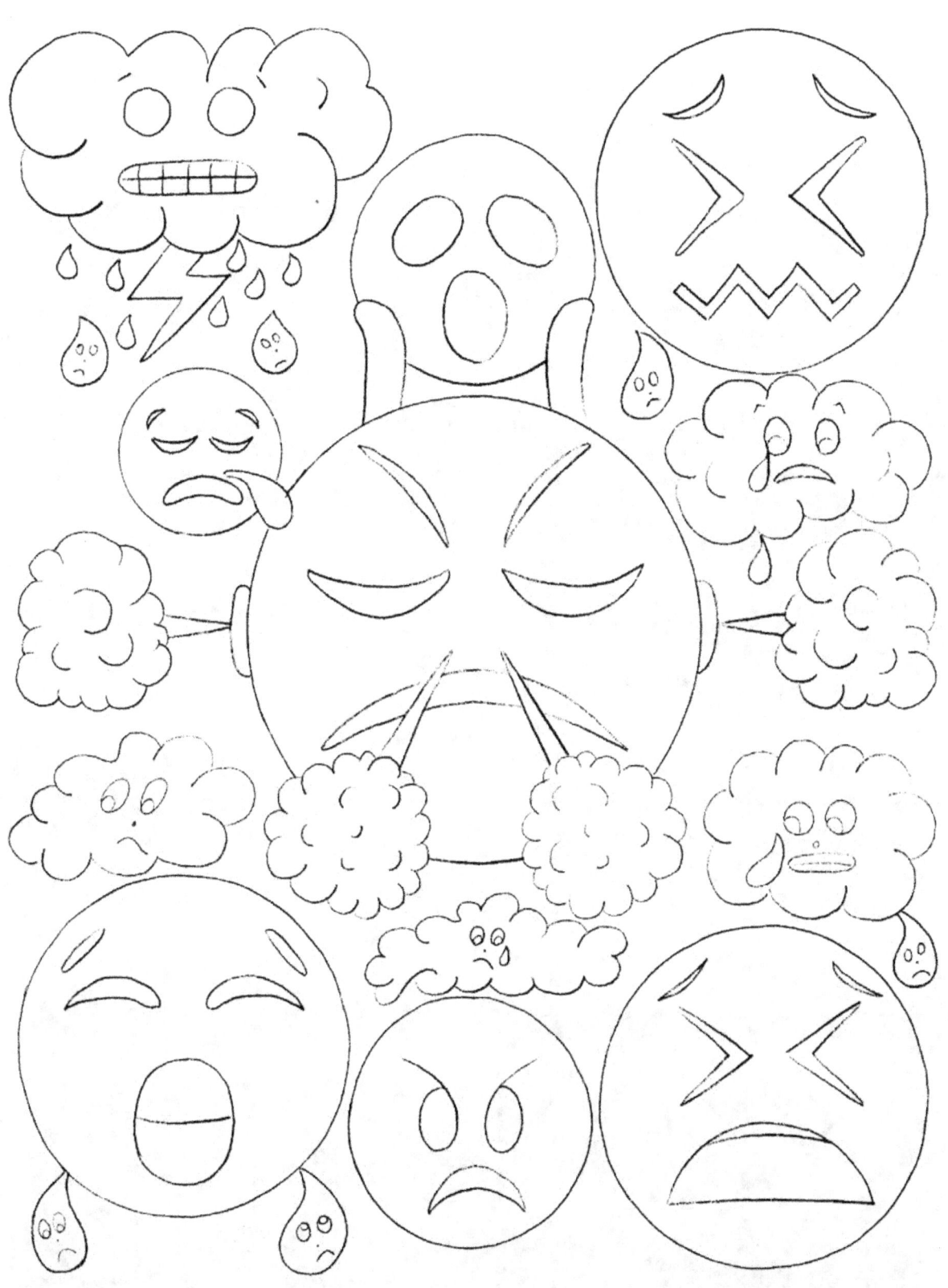

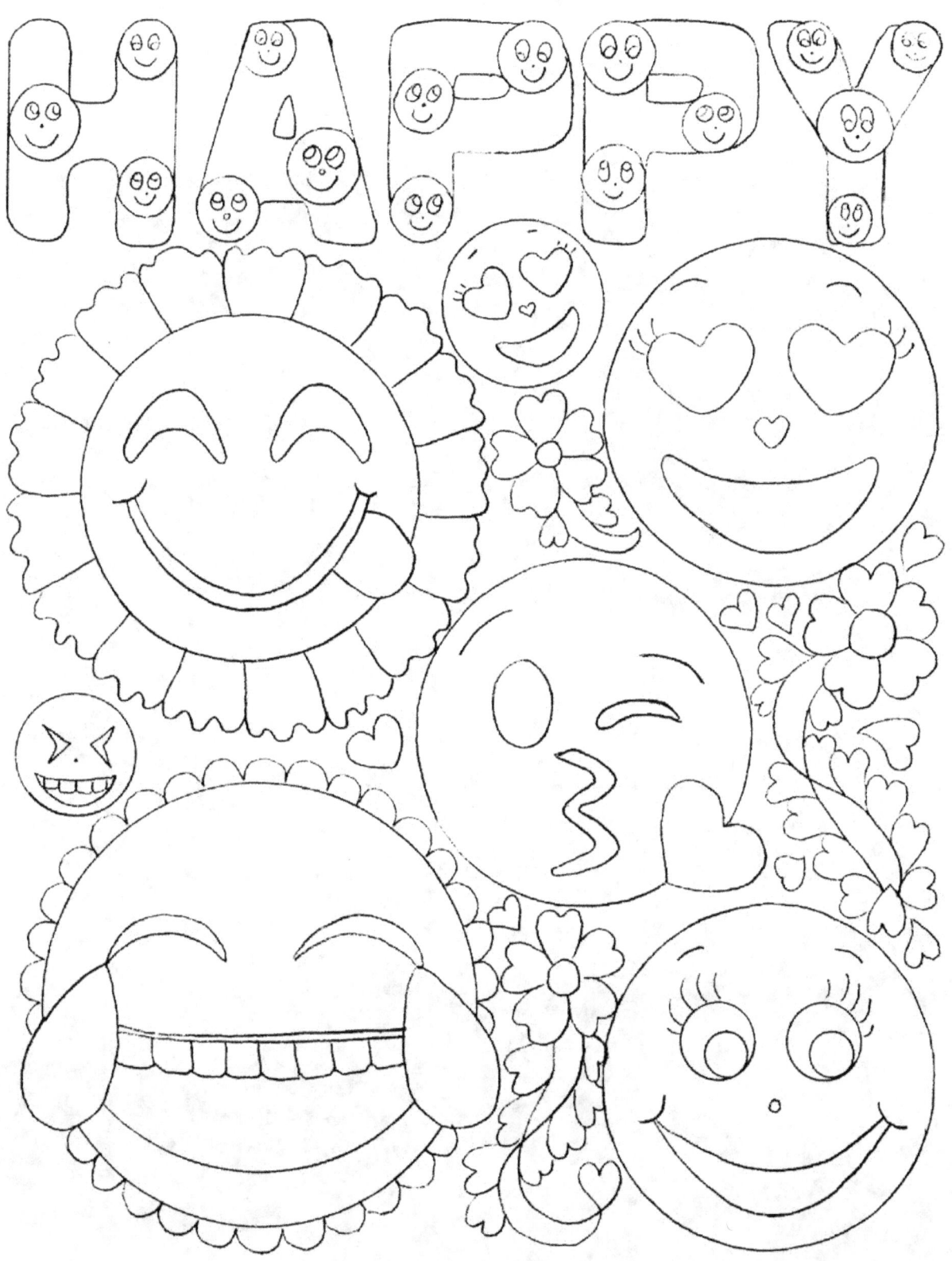

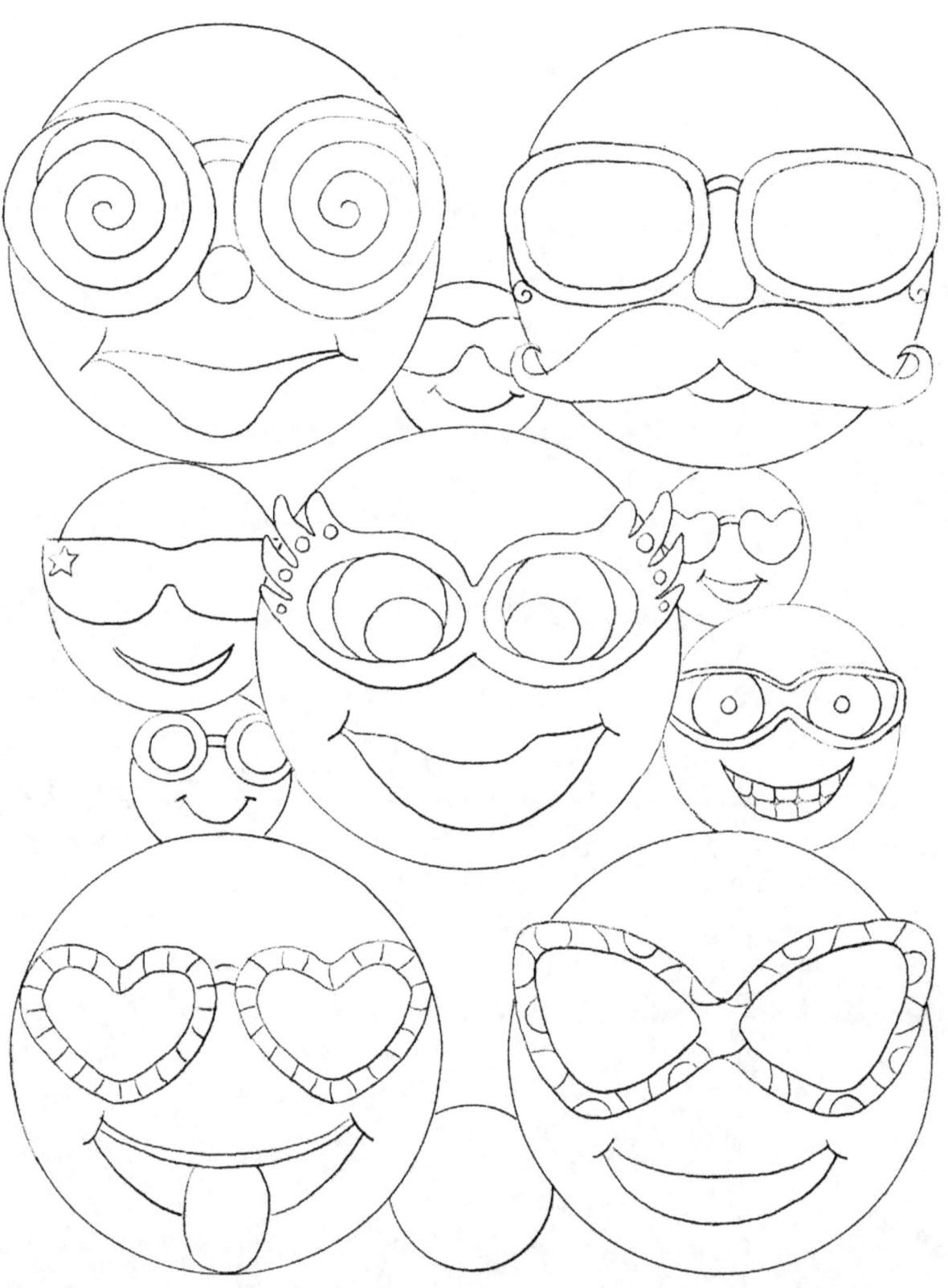

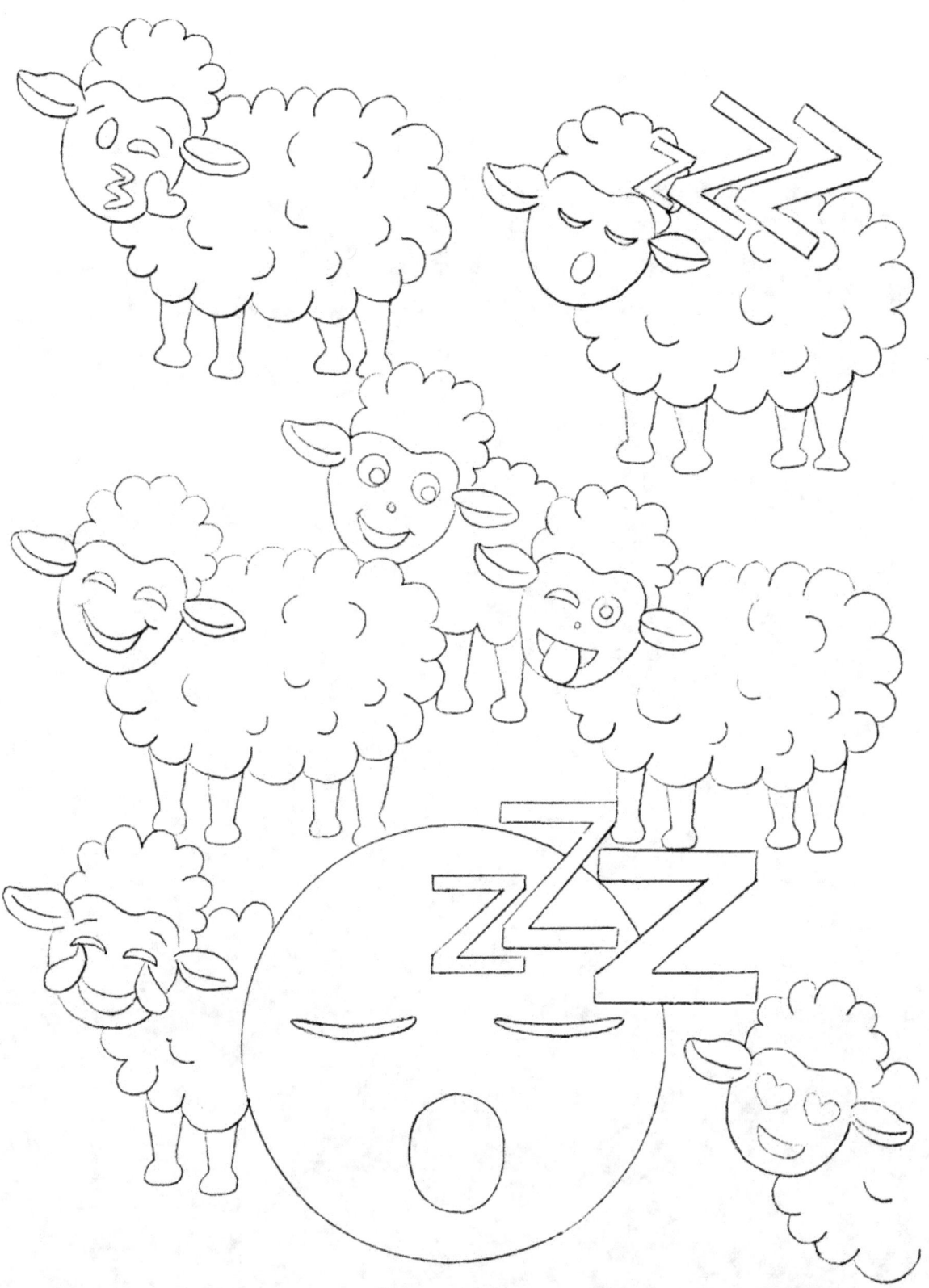

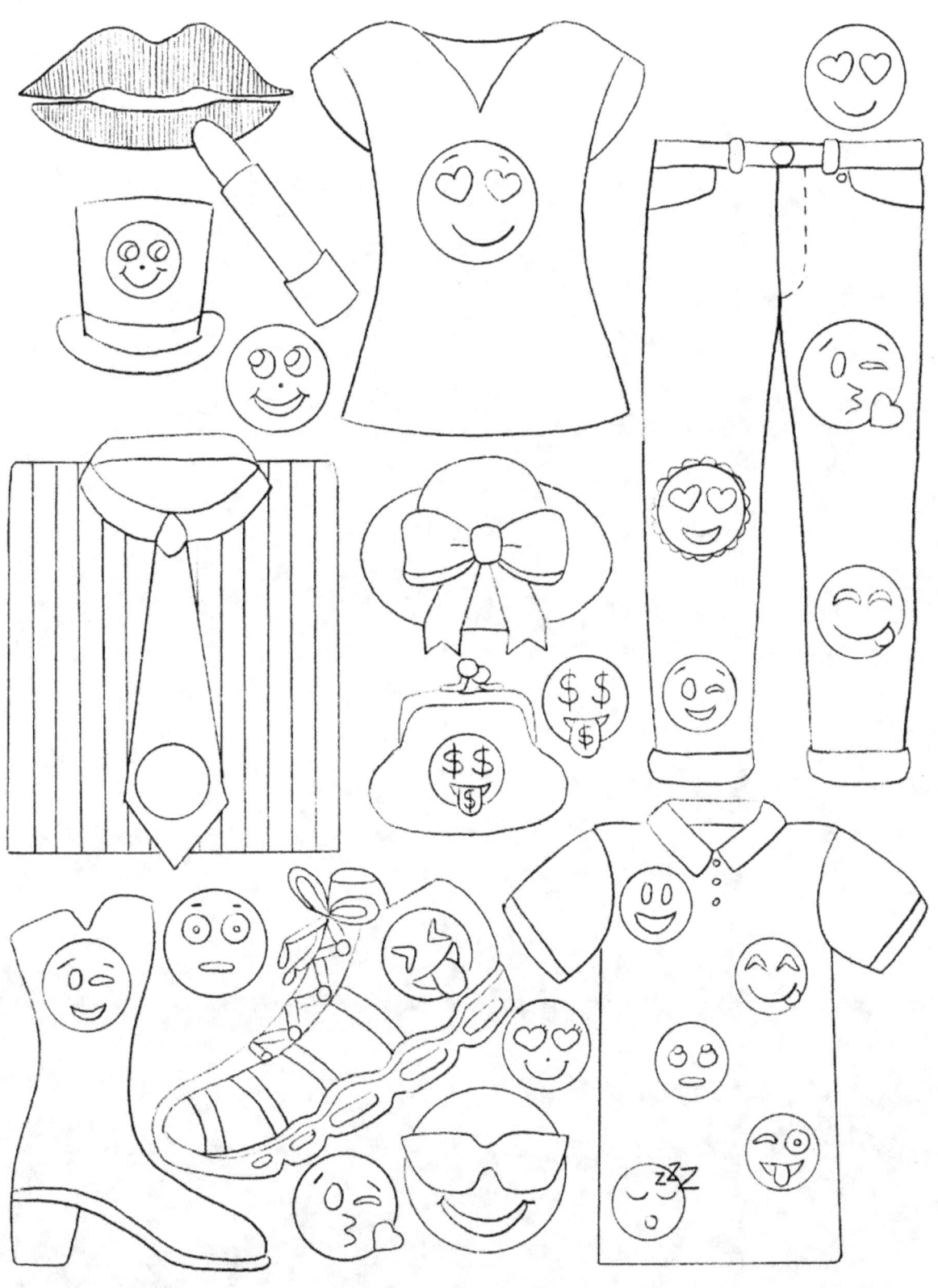

On the blank face, draw and color an emoji that describes your BFF.

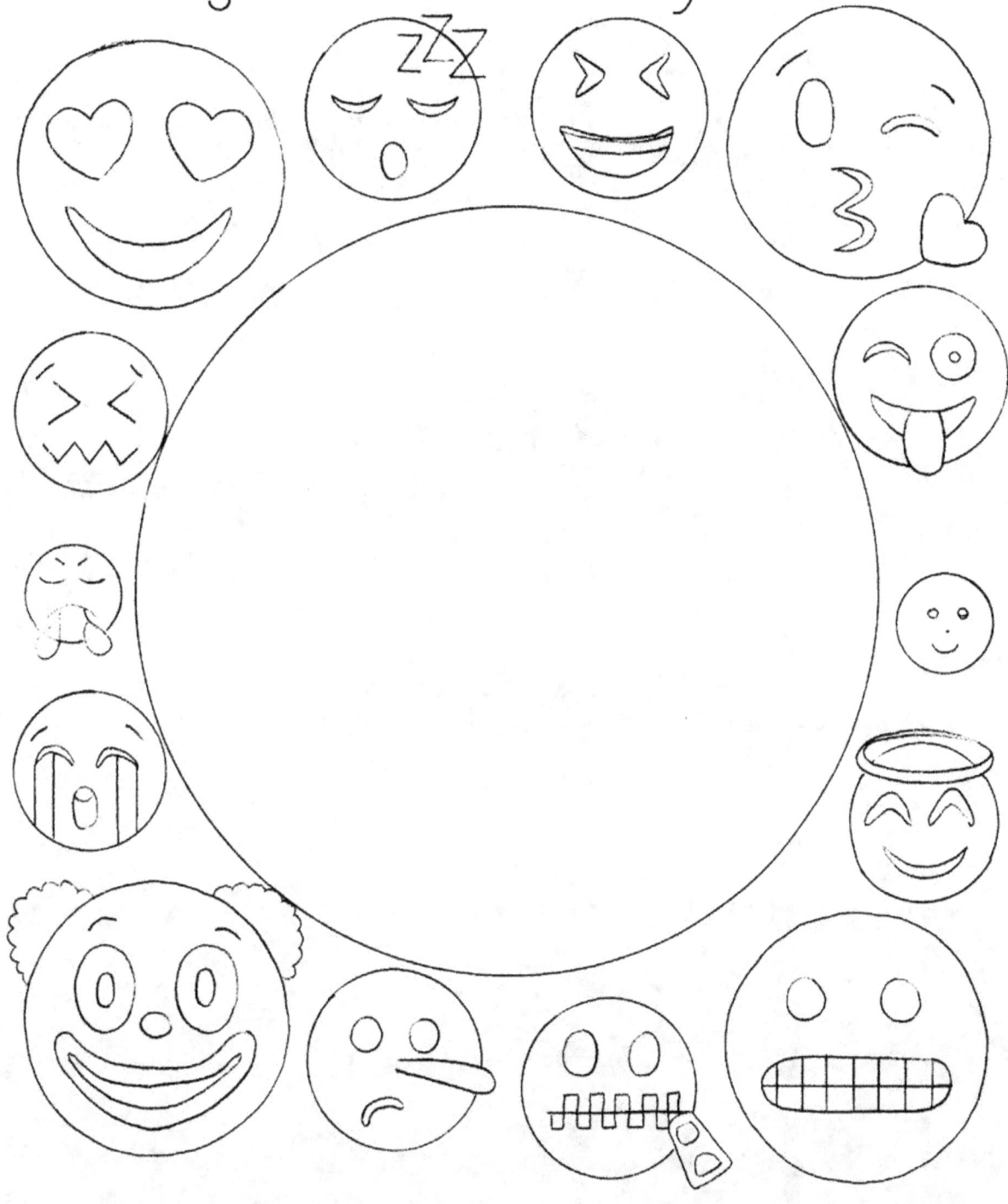

DESIGN YOUR OWN EMOJI

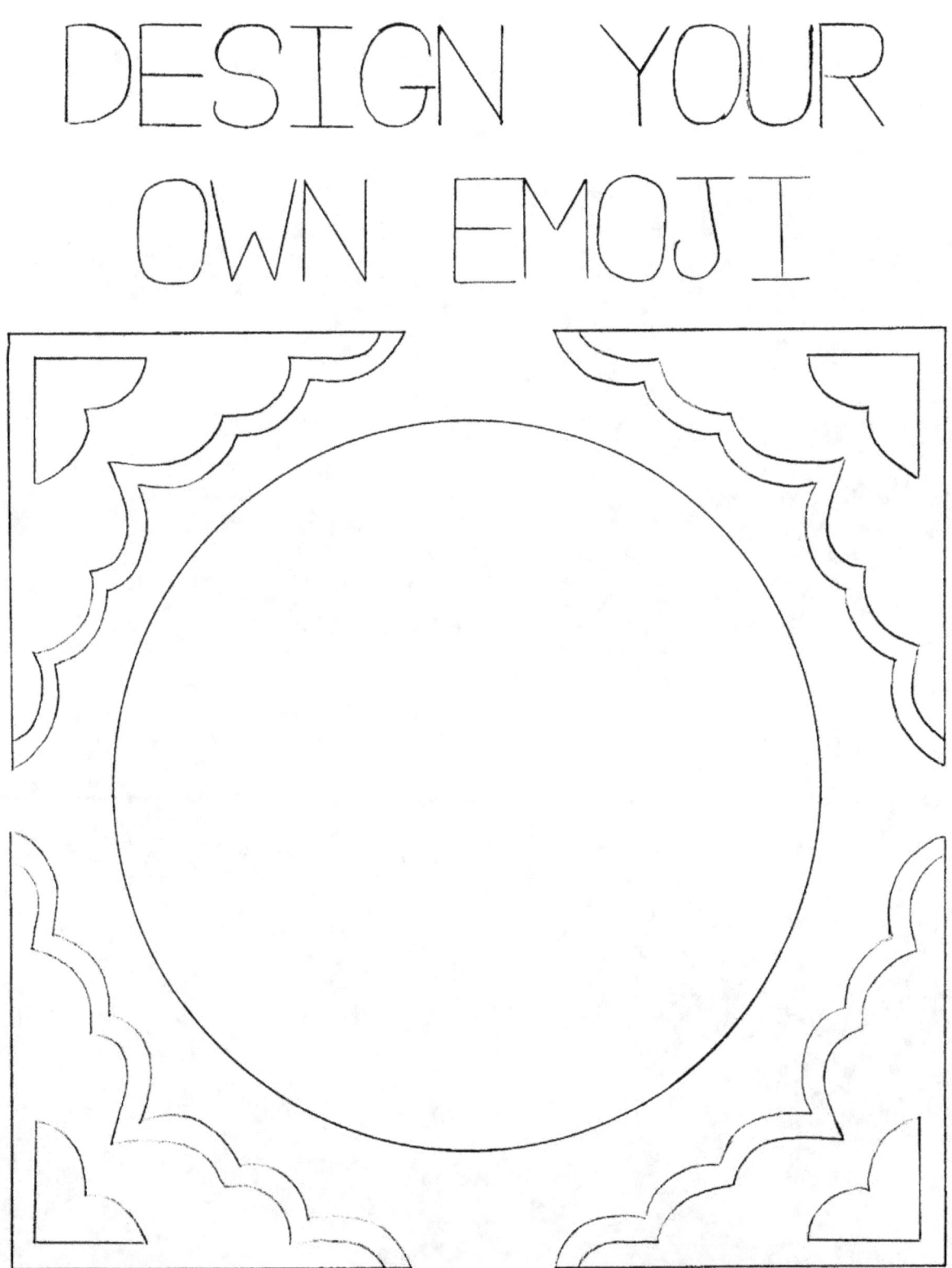

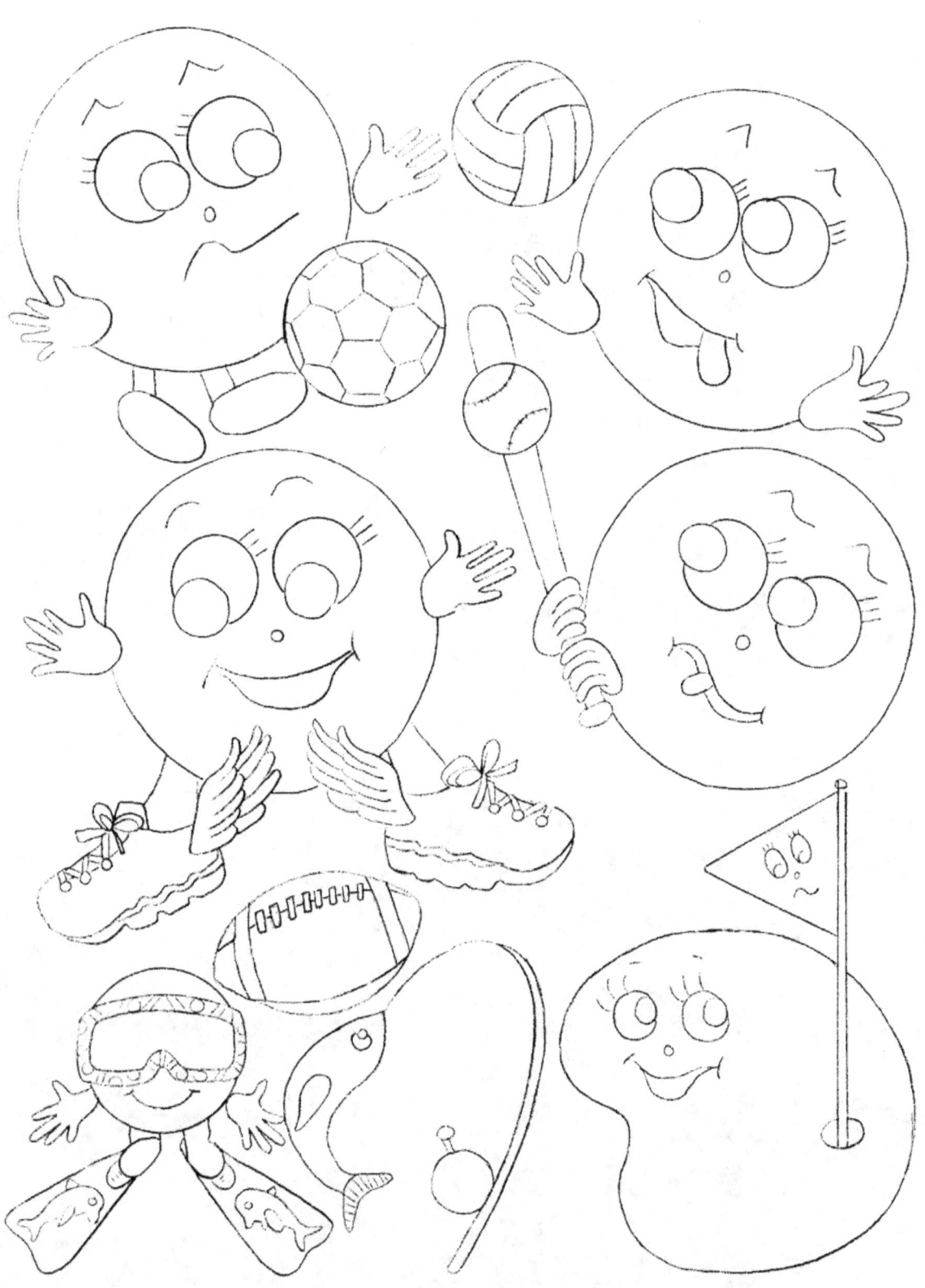

DRAW YOUR NINE FAVORITE EMOJIS

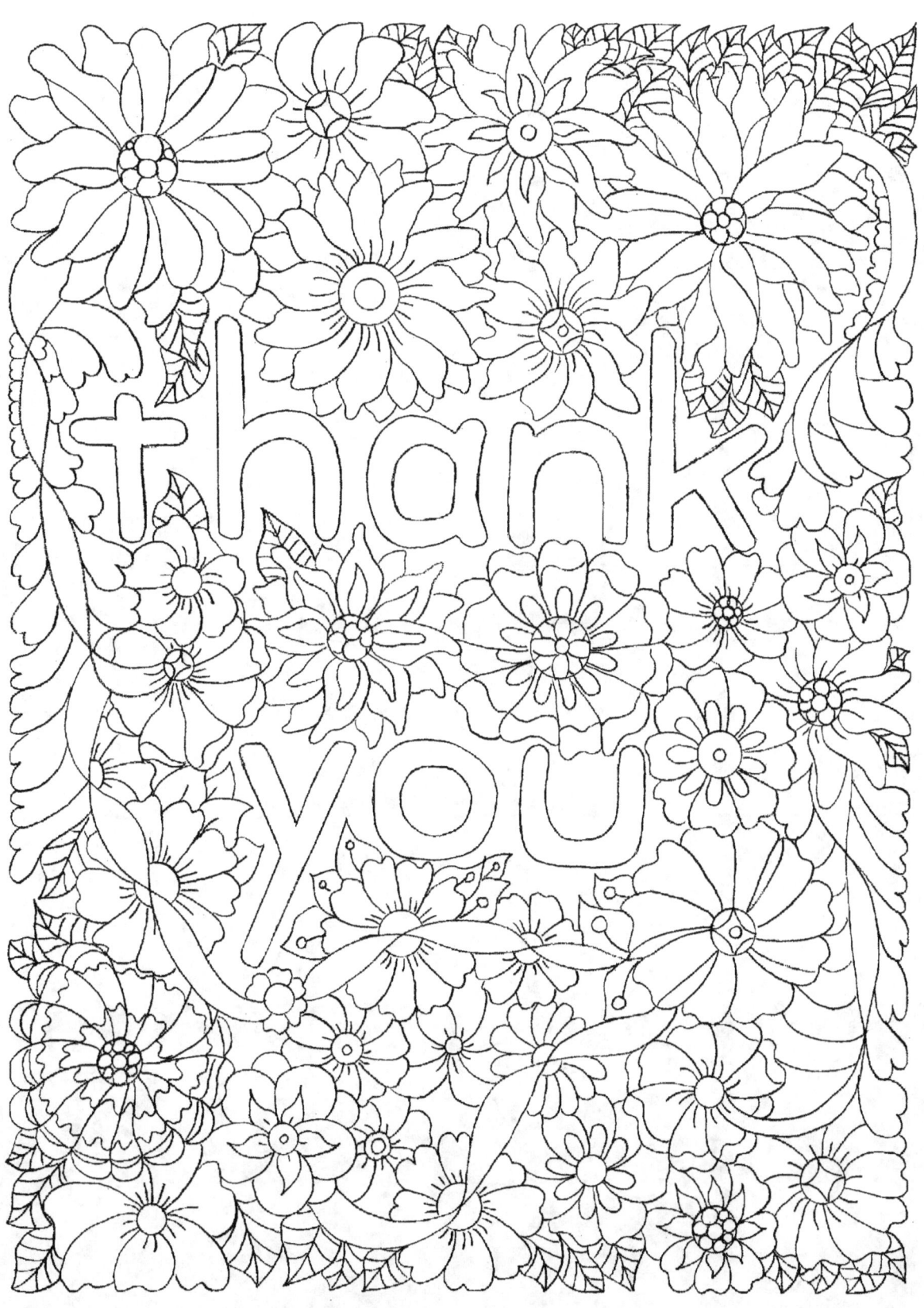

www.ingramcontent.com/pod-product-compliance
Lightning Source LLC
Chambersburg PA
CBHW081736220526
45468CB00008B/2130